Christ or the Casino
The Error of the Prosperity
Gospel Message
Danny R. Hollins, PhD

Copyright © 2018 Danny R Hollins, PhD.

All rights reserved. No part of this publication may be reproduced, distributed, or transmitted in any form or by any means, including photocopying, recording, or other electronic or mechanical methods, without the prior written permission of the publisher, except in the case of brief quotations embodied in critical reviews and certain other noncommercial uses permitted by copyright law. For permission requests, write to the publisher, addressed "Attention: Permissions Coordinator," at the address below.

ISBN: 978-0-692-09134-0 (Paperback)
ISBN: 978-0-692-09134-0 (Hardcover)
Copyright © 2018 Danny R Hollins

All rights reserved. This book or any portion thereof may not be reproduced or used in any manner whatsoever without the express written permission of the publisher except for the use of brief quotations in a book review.

Printed by DiggyPOD, Inc., in the United States of America.

First printing, 2018.

Danny R. Hollins
Danny Ray Hollins Ministries
155 Fairfield Drive
Jackson, MS 39206

Contents

CHAPTER ONE
A Culture of Materialism
7

CHAPTER TWO
Casinos Will Be Casinos
29

CHAPTER THREE
Striking Similarities
38

CHAPTER FOUR
The Serious Business of Ministry
49

CHAPTER FIVE
Manipulation by Misuse and Misapplication
68

CHAPTER SIX
Stolen Identity
88

CHAPTER SEVEN
The Character of the Message of Christ
101

CHAPTER EIGHT
Getting Back On Message
115

Endnotes

Foreword

In Dr. Danny R. Hollins' thought-provoking and timely book, ***Christ or the Casino: The Error of the Prosperity Gospel Message***, I was appreciatively impressed and mesmerized by its thesis and the eloquent and erudite way in which that thesis was presented.

The thesis: Dr. Hollins perceptively and correctly maintains that the "health and wealth" prosperity movement, which has so dubiously helped to produce what he calls the "casino age message," has seriously seduced large numbers of Christians into believing that Christ is some kind of *sanctified ATM machine*, consequently, causing many believers to forget that, in the words of Dr. Hollins himself, "The answer is not in the coins but in the Christ."

Dr. Danny Ray Hollins, who I am terribly proud to call my friend, has written a penetrating and masterful manuscript that challenges all of us who are Christians to become more determined to heed and obey the words of our Lord when He declared, "But seek ye first the Kingdom of God, and his righteousness, and all these things shall be added unto you" (Matthew 6:33).

Humbly Submitted,

Manuel Scott, Jr.
National Evangelist

National Evangelist Manuel Scott, Jr. has published a new book, ***The Quotable Manuel Scott Sr: Words From A Gospel Genius***. "Don't crown your heroes too soon." Just one of nearly 500 quotations by the late Dr. Manuel Scott Sr, who was twice named one of "*America's 15 Greatest Black Preachers*" by **Ebony** magazine. Order your copy today at http://www.manuelscottjr.org/

Preface

One might ask why write a book and entitle it "Christ or the Casino." Why the casino? The pure message of our Savior is increasingly being contaminated by those who advocate a message that has material prosperity as its central theme. The message is masked with the Name of Jesus to give it the appearance of authenticity like a pun in a casino. Jesus is being used as a part of a game to take advantage of people who are vulnerable because of faithlessness, covetousness and a warped approach in their understanding of God's word. Essentially, it is a "Quick Fix", "Get Rich Quick," "Name it and Claim it," message without any challenge toward obedience or endorsement of the servant and selfless aspects that our Lord calls us to.

There are about fifteen hundred casinos, horse tracks, dog tracks or resorts of some kind in the country. There are also over two thousand online gambling sites, not to include bingo parlors and all types of lotteries. Gambling is and always has been very much a part of our culture. This book, however, is not written to give insight to or to discredit casinos. Obviously, because we are people of the Christian faith, and believers in the Bible as God's word, we take a position in opposition to the purpose and activity of casinos. The book begins with the premise that we already believe that the just shall live by faith, and gambling as a means of making a living is sinful. So, I am not endeavoring to argue for or buttress what is already established Christian doctrine. Conversely, this book is written with a concern for the obnoxious and tragic way the gospel is used for self-interest and material gain.

The Apostle Paul admonishes us in Romans 12:2, "Be not conformed to this world…" Here, Paul means becoming fashioned to this world's customs and traditions. Not only are we conforming, the customs and traditions have begun seeping into Christian ministries around the world. Ministries are becoming more about gaming and exploitation, as opposed to the promulgation of Christ's message. A relevant question to ask is, "if Christ showed up in some of our worship events, would he be comfortable being present? Would he be at ease with some of the language being used in services that bear his name? Would he be content with observing as some of the appeals are made from the sacred altar, where men and women of God stand with a solemn obligation to proclaim the unadulterated gospel of Jesus Christ? "

Before our Lord stepped on the cloud and disappeared into glory, he commissioned us to be his witnesses and to spread his gospel message to the ends of the earth. For it is incumbent upon every follower of his, particularly preachers and teachers, to promote his message with zeal and accuracy. When that message is perverted, intentionally or unintentionally, the Lord's plan is hindered, and we should be provoked to raise a standard against this perversion. This book looks at how the materialist ways of this present culture, referred to in the book as the Casino Age, and how they are increasingly being adopted by the Christian Church. This book draws a comparison between the similarities within casinos and the methods of those who advance the message of health, wealth and prosperity. This book considers the exploitive techniques of both, that results from a basis of self-gain and gratification. Further, this book reveals how scripture is misinterpreted and misused to undergird this unsound doctrine, and presents a more accurate scriptural interpretation.

A Prayer

Father, thank you for Jesus, whom you gave so unconditionally to vicariously give his life on Calvary's cross for everyone who comes into this world. Lord, we understand that you have charged us who are saved through his sacrifice, and members of his universal church, to proclaim to this lost world your glorious message of the cross, that men may be reconciled back to you. Lord, as we live here in this world with everything you created for our convenience, help us not to be lured into the temptation of mixing the Gospel Message with any illicit desire for this world's treasures. Help us Lord, to enthusiastically share the Good News purely and without ambiguity in Jesus Name, Amen!

Chapter I
A Culture of Materialism

"For the love of money is the root of all evil: which while some coveted after, they have erred from the faith, and pierced themselves through with many sorrows. But thou, O man of God, flee these things; and follow after righteousness, godliness, faith, love, patience, meekness" I Timothy 6:10-11.

We live now in a culture of materialism, one that is dominated by greed and covetousness. Jesus admonishes us to be on guard against covetousness in Luke 12:15, and Paul warns Timothy of the dangers of the love of money in I Timothy 6:10-11. It is the insatiable appetite that drives this selfish and proud mentality, which ends with the perpetuation of evil. This age is characterized by a low premium on the ethic of work so that it is no longer about working hard but getting rich quick without work.

Recently, I read an article on the Internet where a man was reported missing after winning 30 million dollars in the lottery and was presumed to be dead. From all indications, he was being hounded by some of his friends who greedily saw opportunities for themselves. In 2009, our nation and the world saw us near the edge of going over the proverbial cliff with the failure of financial institutions. We have not yet recovered from that collapse even today in 2015. This was obviously brought about by the lying and scheming actions of the few, thereby creating much pain and woe for many.

Present day economists have called, what led up to the crisis of 2009, the "Casino Economy." It's an economy based on gaming. If you are on the inside, you know what the game is, but many on the outside get caught in a trap because they dare to trust the system. Whereas some trusted the system, many tried to beat it because they were overly anxious to get rich and therefore made themselves vulnerable to gamers. Like those who frequent casinos, the vulnerable distorted reality and only saw what they chose to see. This made them prime prey for the gamers. A recent example of such vulnerability exists in the Madoff scandal.

Bernard "Bernie" Madoff's name became infamous because of his ability to scam millions. He used a technique named after Charles Ponzi in the early 1920s called a **Ponzi** scheme. Ponzi, an Italian who cleverly schemed many out of their investments, convinced them to invest their hard earned money into his deceitful game enabling him to get rich quick. Borrowing Ponzi's methods, Madoff took money from his last investors and gave it to his first investors, inducing a false euphoric feeling of quick return. Because investors were given money in hand, they felt a degree of hope which kept them giving. This enabled Madoff to make off with millions of his investors' dollars.

The current era in which we live is unquestionably one where the actions of so many are driven by an exigent *lust* for material wealth. It confirms the words of the Apostle Paul to Timothy.

> "But they that will be rich fall into temptation and a snare, and into many foolish and hurtful lusts, which drown men in destruction and perdition. For the love of money is the root of all evil: which while some coveted after, they have erred from the faith, and pierced themselves through with many sorrows." I Timothy 6:10

The term lust is often defined much too narrowly. It is purported in the written and spoken language as being synonymous with sexual appetite. But there is a world of ills that are perpetuated because of this salacious behavior, because lust is the raging appetite of the human flesh. Simply put, whatever you have a strong, passionate or overmastering desire and craving for is lust. That can be money, power, alcohol, drugs, and even sex, but not limited to either. The thievery and illicit acts of the sort perpetrated by Madoff, Ponzi, and yes, even ministries are germinated in the evil, yet fertile soil of lustful appetites. It is this lust that drives actions, destroys individuals and breeds conflict among people. James confirmed this in the bible for us when he wrote:

> "From whence come wars and fightings among you? come they not hence, even of your lusts that war in your members? Ye lust, and have not: ye kill, and desire to have, and cannot obtain: ye fight and war, yet ye have not, because ye ask not. Ye ask, and receive not, because ye ask amiss, that ye may consume it upon your lusts." James 4:1-3

The Church's Mandate

The Church is the one entity that God has placed in this world to bring change, set the standard for living, and speak on behalf of the misused and abused, which is a part of its God given mandate. It is not unheard of in this age for the most vulnerable to be taken advantage of. Many, in the winter of their lives, are attacked physically, homes broken into, and maltreated in various ways. There appears to be no value or respect for human life, young or old. Today, there seems to be only respect for the rule of money. Much of the world's present financial crisis finds many upside down in their mortgages because they lust for and try to grab hold to more than they can afford. The work ethic has been totally replaced by an ethic that suggests one can have what one wants despite the lack of sacrifice, discipline or good stewardship. What's even sadder is that the church has, in part, drifted into embracing or at least enabling this phenomenon.

We are neglecting our number one mandate, which is the Great Commission in which Jesus commands us to convert and make disciples of men (Matthew 28:16-20). Furthermore, in the great Sermon on the Mount, Jesus instructed his followers, the church, that it is our responsibility to change the world.

> "You are the salt of the earth. But if the salt loses its saltiness, how can it be made salty again? It is no longer good for anything, except

to be thrown out and trampled by men. You are the light of the world. A city on a hill cannot be hidden. Neither do people light a lamp and put it under a bowl. Instead, they put it on its stand, and it gives light to everyone in the house. In the same way, let your light shine before men, that they may see your good deeds and praise your Father in heaven." Matthew 5:13-16 (New International Version)

What a clear indictment on us by the word of our Lord. Salt is used here by Jesus as a metaphor to suggest that we are to essentially be in the business of world preservation. In the day of Jesus, and today, the world experiences a large degree of corruption and decay. Day by day this world is proverbially going to "Hell in a hand basket". Traditional values that at one time weren't questionable as the rule are more and more seen as the exception. We, the Lord's *Called and Elect*, the Church of the Lord Jesus, and the *salt* of the earth, are commissioned to make a positive difference in the world.

Growing up on a farm in Pocahontas, Mississippi, my family raised hogs as a means of helping to keep food on the table. It was like a holiday when it was time to kill hogs and I along with my other siblings were gaiety with glee. Rising up early with my brothers on those brisk winter mornings, we watched our daddy set things in order for hog slaughtering. After the hog had been slaughtered, hung and cleaned, it was laid on a table and cut into pieces. The hams, the shoulders, ribs and other parts were all separated apart and laid in a wooden box on the inside of a smokehouse. The first time I got a chance to witness this, I remember seeing boxes of brown salt lying on the ground. I asked my dad, "What is it going to be used for?" He said, "Boy, we gon put that salt on the hog." I asked him the second time, "Well, why do we need to put salt on the hog?" He said these words, "The salt will help the hog keep." I didn't know what that meant so I then asked for clarity. "The salt keeps the meat from spoiling," he said. The smokehouse, where the meat was kept, was outside and was stored there through the winter and even through summer months. The meat never spoiled because the salt preserved it. Comparatively, when Jesus tells the church, that we are the salt of the earth, he intends to relay to us an undeniable message that we are the agents that he uses to keep this world from going into decay.

Now, one needs not look very far from where he lives or works to see that we are failing in our responsibility. All over the country and the world, we see decay. Although we are a part of the Church of the Lord Jesus Christ, and called to be light and salt, we are concealing our light and our salt has become insipid. The power of our influence has been diminished because we've allowed the world to shape our actions as opposed to us shaping theirs. Rather than embracing this magnanimous challenge that Jesus has given us, we, in many instances, are promoting greed through the misapplied message of prosperity preaching. If we have been called into ministry, we are to be stewards of the gospel message of Jesus Christ, which means that we are to advocate a message that is meant to change the world and not engage in activity that is more indicative of the unchanged world.

It is not a difficult thing for us to know what the mandate of the church should be; it is no mystery. In fact, all we have to do is consult the one who instituted it and then follow what he tells us to do. In Matthew 16:18, Jesus says to the Apostle Peter, "Upon this rock I will build my church and the gates of hell shall not prevail against it". Now, the last time I checked, "my" is a possessive pronoun that implies ownership. The church belongs to Christ and his message that should be paramount.

The seriousness of this matter can really be seen in the actions of Jesus after he entered Jerusalem for the final time. Having had his triumphant entry on the back of a young donkey, Jesus went into the temple and he was troubled by what he saw. Mark 15 says that he saw the exchangers of money, cheating people, misusing the poor and making his house something other than what it is meant to be. This is the one time in scripture that we observe Jesus literally angry. He picked up a switch of sorts and began turning over the tables of the money changers and drove them out of the temple. After having done that, he uttered these famous words, "It is written that my house shall be called the house of prayer but ye have made it a den of thieves".

Would Jesus Be Comfortable
    It's quite sad, but if Jesus walked into some of our assemblies today and observed what's going on, he'd be forced to pick up his switch again, and drive some people out. The church is not a place for scheming and games but a place where the Lord is to be glorified in his house. "But if I tarry long, that thou mayest know how thou oughtest to behave thyself in the house of God, which is the church of the living God, the pillar and ground of the truth" (I Timothy 3:15). Some years ago, when I served as pastor in a small area in Pocahontas, a senior lady told me something that was quite profound and relevant to this issue. "When I go to church I want to feel like I've been to church," she said. My daddy put it this way, "Even the wino on the corner, when he goes to church, knows when he is really in church." How often have we heard this?

    Bring me $500 if you want your deliverance. Sow into this ministry a $1,000 and you will become debt free. Give me this, that or the other amount if you really want God to move for you.

    The problem with this kind of doctrine is that it makes null and void what Jesus has already done; the price has already been paid. When Jesus died on Calvary's cross he paid our sin debt in full. Whatever we will get from God now or in the future, is already covered in the blood of Calvary's cross. In the previous passage cited where Jesus went into the temple, and drove out the moneychangers, an interesting happened. Those who were lame, blind and had other infirmities, came in and he healed them. There was no money offered, no $500 or $1,000 lines; just simply Jesus healing as he willed to do so.

There can be nothing said to us clearer about the mandate of Jesus Christ for his church than that of his last words before he ascended to the Father. In Matthew 28:18-20, we find what is termed to be the Great Commission. It is the command that is given to the universal church relative to its responsibility while Christ is away. It reads, "All power in heaven and earth is in my hand, go ye therefore and teach all nations, baptizing them in the name of the Father, and of the Son, and of the Holy Ghost: Teaching them to observe all things whatsoever I have commanded you: and, lo, I am with you always, even unto the end of the world."

The Pearl of Great Price

Matthew 13 records the words of Jesus in his parable of the Pearl of Great Price. It speaks of a certain merchant who is seeking pearls and finds one of great value. He sold all he had to purchase that special pearl. Jesus is that pearl, and he's enough all by himself. We are to be consumed with the matter of making disciples for the kingdom of Christ, in contrast to making disciples rich within the kingdom of Christ. We are rich already in Jesus. Jesus said further to his followers, "…and you shall be my witnesses in Jerusalem, in Judea, in Samaria and in the uttermost parts of the earth" (Acts 1:8). Yes, witnesses! The word witness carries with it the connotation of a martyr, one who gives his life for another as a testimony for another. All the original disciples of Jesus did just that! They laid down their lives because Jesus was the most important person to them.

There is nowhere written in the New Testament, particularly from the ascension of Jesus to the end of the Bible, where any of his disciples or his followers, were consumed with becoming wealthy or advocated a doctrine of prosperity, especially of the kind that is being advocated in pulpits across the country today. In fact, when we see Peter and John at the end of Pentecost going down to the temple at the hour of prayer, there was a man placed there at the gate called Beautiful. The bible tells us that he was lame from his mother's womb. There he lay, figuratively with a cup in his hand, asking the passersby for a quarter, dime, nickel or penny to help him on his way. Peter and John arrived on the scene and the lame man asked for money. Peter simply said to the man, "Silver and gold have I none but such as I have, give I thee in the Name of Jesus Christ of Nazareth, rise up and walk." I suppose, had the same situation occurred in present day arenas, Peter's words would have been these, "if you sow your seed of $100, $200 or $1,000, you can get your healing." Peter and John knew that the answer was not in the coins but in the Christ. When you have the Christ, you have all you need to make the journey. Charles Price Jones wrote a song that I love to hear and sometimes love to sing, when I am in a singing mood, *"There is nothing more precious than Jesus to me. Let earth with its treasures be gone. I am rich as can be with my Savior I'll see. I'm happy with Jesus alone."*

In the first half of the section of the passage cited previously in Matthew 5, Jesus uses the metaphor salt as the agent meant to be a preservative. Similarly, we are to preserve the world to keep it from decaying. The second half of the passage is equally as profound and important. Jesus says that "We are the light of the world and the city that is on a hill that cannot be hidden. For neither do men light a lamp and put it under a bushel but on a lamp stand that it might give light to the entire house. Let your light so shine," he says, "before men that they may see your good works and glorify the Father which is in heaven." What is Jesus really saying? Light that is being reflected from us is actually Jesus radiating through us. So when the world sees us as representatives of Christ (the Church of the Lord Jesus Christ, the called, the elect), they see Jesus. We are the closest thing to what the world will ever see of what Jesus is really like.

This is an awesome responsibility, which means that we have to be very careful that we represent him in the truest sense. All over this land, darkness seems to prevail. James Weldon Johnson, in his poetic selection entitled *The Creation,* describes what the universe looked like just prior to God creating light. He said that "...darkness was everywhere, blacker than a hundred midnights in a cypress swamp." Now,

I don't know whether it is quite that dark today, but I can't imagine it being any darker in Christian ministry with the message of Christ being perverted and changed into a message that is about satisfaction of self and manipulating God. It is dark! When it is dark, no one asks the question, "Where is the darkness?" but "Where is the light?" Jesus has quite clearly told us what the light is and who the light is. We are the light of the world and this dark world is crying out for light to be made manifest. What is sadder still is that we are doing just what Jesus admonished us not to do. "Neither do men light a light and put it under a bushel but on a lamp stand where it might give light to the whole house." We are putting our lights under the bushels of prosperity preaching, covetousness and greed, and the world continues to be lost and floundering in darkness.

The Changing Culture within the Church

In Webster's Dictionary, culture is defined as the set of shared attitudes, beliefs, values, goals, and practices that characterizes an institution or organization. The church is the body of Christ and we are admonished not to conform to the world's culture, but we do have a culture of our own that we should maintain. Though we are broken down into varying local assemblies, universally we have shared values or norms that make us unique. With the advent of the health, wealth and prosperity doctrine, these values are being undermined, and are now being portrayed as "traditional" and out of touch with what the Lord is doing today.

Normalcy is scoffed at by those who advocate this doctrine and suggests that those who hold to the norms of the church are not allowing the Holy Spirit to work. The declaration is that if one holds to the norm, one denies God's promises to his people. In every area of life, norms are important to determine when something is functioning properly. For example, when one gets sick and goes to the doctor, the nurse or some medical attendant will take our vital signs. Those numbers should fall within a certain range, and are measured against what is accepted as normal vital signs which will govern the doctor's advice to the patient. Surely you have known situations where a person's vitals were so out of range that they were sent directly to the hospital. Indeed, the vital signs reverberating out of the mouths of our messengers within the Christian community are troubling, even critical. This "Casino Age" message that is being promoted is creating disturbing consequences within the body of Christ.

Consequences of the Casino Age Message

Agitation and Dissatisfaction
"But godliness with contentment is great gain." I Timothy 6:6 (King James Version)

Have you ever seen so many agitated and dissatisfied Christians as we are witnessing today? Previously, I recalled growing up on a farm in a very modest situation. I remember well how my parents admonished us always to be thankful for what we had. They repeated over and over again how desperate things were in their day with far less than we have in terms of financial and material wealth. Although families essentially survived off the land, they were as happy and content as could be. Would a little money here or there have been a big help in making things more convenient? Yes, but they were not consumed with the absence of it.

Christians today are agitated not just because of what they don't have, but what they don't have that others do have. The prevailing problem is that the world has become our standard for comparison when in reality we should be looking at the standards Christ set forth. The greater conundrum is that the church, in many instances, validates this thwarted view by advancing a message that points to worldly gain as the prominent goal for which one should strive. Asaph, in Psalm 73, seems to struggle with this dilemma.

> "God is truly good to Israel, especially to everyone with a pure heart. But I almost stumbled and fell, because it made me jealous to see proud and evil people and to watch them

prosper…they stay healthy, and they don't have troubles like everyone else. Their pride is like a necklace, and they commit sin more often than they dress themselves…They sneer and say cruel things, and because of their pride, they make violent threats. They dare to speak against God and to order others around…Yet all goes well for them, and they live in peace. What good did it do me to keep my thoughts pure and refuse to do wrong? It was hard for me to understand all this! Then I went to your temple, and there I understood what will happen to my enemies. You will make them stumble, never to get up again. They will be terrified, suddenly swept away and no longer there…" Psalm 73:2-19 (Contemporary English Version)

What a useful and practical passage of scripture. Asaph is unquestionably angry, but with whom? We know it's not with God because he begins this passage acclaiming the goodness of God. I believe that Asaph, like many today, is plagued with the problem of discontentment. He seems to feel that his commitment and faithfulness toward God ought to result in his being rewarded with a trouble free and wealthy life. He observes the wicked, which are not committed to God, doing all sorts of evil deeds. To his sorrow, they are seemingly prospering with no worries, troubles, or trials. As shown in the beginning passage, this was absolutely too difficult for him to understand. But then, he did what all Christians should do each Sunday, he went to the house of the Lord and it was there that he had an awakening. He was given new illumination, on what this all means and how this all works. He seems at that moment to realize that in the scheme of God's providence, all of this works out in the end and that the wicked do not get off free as it seems. God ultimately holds and has the final word. I'm sure Asaph left the temple rejoicing and feeling much better, for his burden had been lifted. When he went home, he no longer had to toss and turn, losing sleep at night because of his discontentment. He was resting well, as he was safe and assured in the fact that God was still God and was indeed enough.

Many Christians across the breadth of this country attend Sunday morning worship and other types of settings where the name of the Lord is being hailed and acclaimed. However, many of them leave having gotten a message that would not provoke the same kind of feeling that Asaph got when he went to the temple. Many messages today lay the foundation for inward conflict by suggesting we can have it if you want it. God wants you to be rich, they say, and have the biggest house in the neighborhood, the most expensive car, and whatever our heart desires. These are the words spoken on a consistent basis from pulpits and arenas across the country. Consequently, when Christians look at others who have these material things, they become discontent and feel like God has neglected them or that God is not enough.

I am reminded of a song that we sang when I was younger growing up and singing in the choir in Pocahontas. *"Some folk would rather have houses and lands, some folk to silver and gold, these things they will treasure and forget about their souls. I have decided to make Jesus my choice."* Lest you get the impression that I am advocating a message that God is against us having the benefit of the enjoyment and conveniences of material things, I want to set the record straight. The Lord is the owner of the cattle on a thousand hills and the scripture tells us that *"the earth is his and the fullest thereof"*. It also says that *"the silver and gold is mine said the Lord"*. We are his children and he is the best father, who showers down upon us bountiful blessings. We must also accept that just as he blesses us, he reserves the right to himself to give to us when he feels necessary and withhold as he wills. Thank God that he knows better than we do. He knows what is best for us.

If one wants to have a good look at what prosperity actually is, look at someone who is righteous. Don't look at the wicked because that is deceptive. The fallacy of this doctrine of materialism is that somehow material prosperity is equated with spirituality. This is unquestionably foolishness on the surface. If this were true, many in the secular world of whom we are familiar would be considered spiritual. Michael Jackson, one of the greatest entertainers that the world has ever known, had millions of dollars, popularity and fame. With that level of success does it mean he should have been considered spiritual or in a close relationship with God? Elvis Presley who is remembered as the king of rock and roll and also one of the greatest entertainers the world has ever known, and had immeasurable riches. Is his success also equated with his spirituality or closeness with God?

The best view of what prosperity looks like is to peek over into the first Psalm of the Holy Scripture. "Blessed is the man that walketh not in the counsel of the ungodly, nor standeth in the way of sinners, nor sitteth in the seat of the scornful. But his delight is in the law of the Lord; and in his law doth he meditate day and night. And he shall be like a tree planted by the rivers of water, that bringeth forth his fruit in his season; his leaf also shall not wither; and whatsoever he doeth shall prosper."

What a beautiful passage, and one of my favorites in the whole Bible. What I like best about this passage is that prosperity is not even talked about until the end of the passage. The Psalmist begins talking about how one is to be blessed or the key to one's happiness and contentment. One is blessed, he says, when one makes a conscious effort to steer away from that which is ungodly and toward that which is godly. He says that one is content and happy when he chooses to meditate on God's word and honors God. God reciprocates by granting him the peace and joy of his blessings. I love the imagery that is used here - one who is prospering as God wills it, is compared to a tree that has been planted by the waters. It is from the life giving water that represents the Almighty God, where the tree has been anchored. It is there that it gets nutrients and necessary food to be vibrant, fresh and full of vigor. You and I represent that tree if we choose to believe that God is enough and are faithful to him and his will for our lives. We don't have to worry about prospering; he will ensure that takes place.

Greed as a Virtue

But they that will be rich fall into temptation and a snare, and into many foolish and hurtful lusts, which drown men in destruction and perdition.   I Timothy 6:9

Another consequence of the casino type message of health, wealth and prosperity is that greed has become a virtue. It is seen as a good thing and morally acceptable. Mark Skousen, in *Is Greed Good,* along with others, postulates that without greed, our current economic and social structures would implode. They suggest that it is a consistent human motivation that stirs economic activity. This type thinking perhaps is acceptable in the secular kingdoms of the world because that's the way the world works. But Christians do not live by the same standards. Our standards are not set by some professor at a university or an economist on Wall Street. Born again children of God are to yield themselves to the principles of the Kingdom of Christ and not the principles of this world. Jesus turns the principles of the world on their heads. He asserts that one saves his life by losing it, becomes great by being a servant, gets exalted by being humble and gains treasures in heaven by giving treasures to the poor.

The voice of Jesus is clear in the Sermon on the Mount, pronouncing to us the folly of greed and grasping unrestrainedly after riches.

> "No one can serve two masters. Either he will hate the one and love the other, or he will be devoted to the one and despise the other. You cannot serve both God and Money. Therefore I tell you, do not worry about your life, what you will eat or drink; or about your body, what you will wear. Is not life more important than food, and the body more important than clothes? Look at the birds of the air; they do not sow or

reap or store away in barns, and yet your heavenly Father feeds them. Are you not much more valuable than they? Who of you by worrying can add a single hour to his life? And why do you worry about clothes? See how the lilies of the field grow. They do not labor or spin. Yet I tell you that not even Solomon in all his splendor was dressed like one of these. If that is how God clothes the grass of the field, which is here today and tomorrow is thrown into the fire, will he not much more clothe you, O you of little faith?" Matthew 6:24-30 (New International Version)

"No man can serve two masters," says Jesus. Once I preached a sermon entitled, "Maintaining Integrity with God." We cannot hold to the Lord's hand crying how much we love him as master, while embracing money as master. It is really to figuratively thumb our noses at the Lord. It is foolish, given that the Lord is omniscient and is always conscious of who we are, what we are doing, and our motives for doing what we do. God created all things for us to have dominion over and to enjoy, but will not be second to any of it.

"Charge them that are rich in this world, that they be not high minded, nor trust in uncertain riches, but in the living God, who giveth us richly all things to enjoy." I Timothy 6:17

God declares himself to be a jealous God, which he has every reason to be. We should consider his goodness and His unconditional love, to the point that when we were yet in sin he gave Jesus to die for our transgressions. He provided for our salvation and continues to show his faithfulness as he feeds, clothes and provides shelter for us. No child of God can ever justifiably claim that he has been a negligent father. Yet, we are so quickly drawn to doctrines that advocate embarking upon a quest after the corruptible things of this world, money being chief among them. Consequently, we've become consumed with greed. Should not the promises of the

Lord be enough? When has he failed? Where has he failed? In everything and in every situation, he has been true to his promises. Nothing advocated by the casino age message can compete with his faithfulness.

Interestingly, this modern doctrine actually promotes trust in God in a perverted kind of way. They promulgate a message that promotes a preoccupation with seeking wealth from a God that gives it freely to all who dare to "name it and claim it." While advocating such a message, they do a serious disservice to the saints by admonishing them to trust in what God has not promised, and consequently, saints are set up for inevitable disappointment when what is expected does not manifest itself. Again, the result of such a message is that it encourages those who are deceived by it to trust God for what he has never promised. When we become preoccupied with even the smallest things relative to survival, we infringe upon God's duty and the responsibilities he has reserved to himself regarding his promises toward us. Jesus says, "Therefore I tell you, do not worry about your life, what you will eat or drink…" In short Christians, "chill out." This is not something you need to spend any time concerning yourselves with. Our God is both willing and able to provide for us. "…I will never leave you nor forsake you", says the Lord and that's a promise in Hebrews 13:5. These passages work well when we are able to resign ourselves to a position of contentment with the Lord's provisions for our lives. The problem, and what I am asserting in this book, is that the so-called prosperity doctrine in reality promotes attitudes of discontentment and greed. Further, these two kindred dispositions are promoted as desirable, even needful if one will tap into the resources of God.

Greed is dangerous and at the end of its path is certain destruction. Geoffrey Chaucer of Medieval England wrote a piece of literature called, *The Canterbury Tales*, a collection of stories, within a framed story, set between the period of 1387 and 1400. The characters are a group of thirty people who travel as pilgrims to Canterbury England to the shrine of Thomas à Becket, Archbishop of Canterbury. The pilgrims, who come from all layers of society, tell stories to each other to kill time while they travel. One of my favorites is the Pardoner's Tale. It is a time period devastated by a disease called the Black Death. This was during one of the most horrific pandemics in human history, peaking in Europe between 1348 and 1350. It is widely thought to have been an outbreak of bubonic plague. The Pardoner, a medieval preacher delegated to raise money for religious works, paints a rather convincing story about the dangers of greed. It should also be noted that ironically, it is actually an indictment of his own trickery with his parishioners.

The story captures three riotous young men, who have an affinity for frequenting taverns. These men, angered by the death of many relatives and countrymen due to the plague, foolishly set out to kill Death. After being drunk with wine, and headed on their mission, they ran into a mysterious old man and rudely demanded that he tell them where Death was. He tells them to follow the crooked path; they will find Death under a large tree. Under the tree they found a pot of gold and their sadness turned into great joy. They drew straws to determine who would go to town to get more wine to continue the celebration. The lot fell on the youngest among them. After he left to get wine, the other two devised a plan to be rid of him so as to have the entire treasure for themselves. One would get his attention by wrestling him to the ground, while the other would stab him from behind. Meanwhile, the younger man thought he could have it all to himself if he could get rid of the other two. He then went to the apothecary to get poison which he poured into the wine. When he returned, one of them playfully rushed him while the other stabbed him in his back and he died. With glee, the two rejoiced, opened the wine and began to drink. After tasting it they too died. This, the Pardoner says, is the reward of gluttony.

A MEistic Mentality

"Yea, they are greedy dogs which can never have enough, and they are shepherds that cannot understand: they all look to their own way, every one for his gain, from his quarter." Isaiah 56:11

Once I heard a very good friend of mine preaching. While making his points, he paused as if he had a loss for words, and then blurted out a word that I was sure could not be found anywhere in the dictionary. He quickly said to a wondering audience "A preacher has the right to make up words." I have taken that same liberty here with the word "MEistic Mentality." A mindset that is purely focused on gratification of me, myself and I, is the definition that I would ascribe to my new word. This casino oriented message has consequentially led to a selfish mindset among us, which has led to behavior that is not conducive to functioning within civilized society, and surely not among Christians.

Charles Darwin, in his book *The Origin of the Species*, advocates something called the survival of the fittest in which the species is engaged in a competitive struggle for existence. This struggle is primarily an essential struggle for food to support growth and life. It's known as the Darwinian evolutionary ethics, which teaches conquering the weak through struggle and survival of self. Christian ethics conversely, teach self-sacrifice and love for ones fellowman, and support of the weak for survival of the whole. The quest for money that many aggressively engage in mirrors actions that closely resemble this survival of the fittest mentality. Money, per se, isn't evil; it is the love of money that gets us into trouble. How we get it and how we use it is the key. When the motives within the Christian church are selfish beyond our own needs, and money is used to give us dominion over our fellows, we are surely out of step with the principles of the kingdom. Our actions are more akin to Darwinian ethics as oppose to Christian; it's the Law of the Jungle. When Moses returned from Mount Sinai with the Ten Commandments, he found the people worshiping a golden calf. In our worship of money, are we not doing the same?

A proper view of what behavior should be among civilized human beings, particularly within the Kingdom of

Christ, is the picture Jesus paints in the popular parable "The Good Samaritan."

> "And Jesus answering said, A certain man went down from Jerusalem to Jericho, and fell among thieves, which stripped him of his raiment, and wounded him, and departed, leaving him half dead. And by chance there came down a certain priest that way: and when he saw him, he passed by on the other side. And likewise a Levite, when he was at the place, came and looked on him, and passed by on the other side. But a certain Samaritan, as he journeyed, came where he was: and when he saw him, he had compassion on him, And went to him, and bound up his wounds, pouring in oil and wine, and set him on his own beast, and brought him to an inn, and took care of him And on the morrow when he departed, he took out two pence, and gave them to the host, and said unto him, Take care of him; and whatsoever thou spendest more, when I come again, I will repay thee. Which now of these three, thinkest thou, was neighbour unto him that fell among the thieves? And he said, He that shewed mercy on him. Then said Jesus unto him, Go, and do thou likewise." Luke 10:30-37

"Go and do likewise," says the Master! Man's concern for mankind is the order of the kingdom. Cain asked a question, *"Am I my brother's keeper?"* It was a sarcastic response to the question God raised as to the whereabouts of his brother, Abel. The answer is clearly laid out in the passage above. If the Law of the Jungle or The Survival of the Fittest had prevailed on the Jericho road, the wounded man would have died.

The parable also pictures the inaction and indifference of the religious community, who should have as its primary cause, the salvation of man. The priest and the Levite do not represent messengers of Satan. These were religious people, synonymous with leaders within the church. The priest was a leader in the church, who was responsible for attending to the atonement of the people, and the Levite was one of the assistants in the house of the Lord. However, it was the hated half breed Samaritan that showed mercy. One cannot have compassion if one is consumed with self. Jesus also sets forth the principle that what he blesses us with is not to be used exclusively on ourselves. *We should not be our own ministry;* for God blesses us to be a blessing to others. The MEistic way of thinking is incompatible with real Christianity.

A Culture of Materialism
Points of Emphasis

- The concern and mandate of the Christ Church is to make disciples after Jesus as commanded in the Great Commission to preserve a decaying world through its powerful influence. (Matthew 28:16-20; Mathew 5:13-16)

- The vital signs of the church relative to its mission, suggest that there is a disturbing move away from the normalcy of the true Christian message to more of a message akin to practices of a casino.

- The casino type gospel message fosters adverse behavior among Saints.

    - Agitation and Dissatisfaction (Psalm 73)
    - Greed as a Virtue (Matthew 6:24-30)
    - A MEistic mindset (Isaiah 56:11)

- Christian Ethics is being substituted for a type of Darwinian Ethics.

Chapter II
Casinos Will Be Casinos

    In this section, I'll briefly discuss prevailing activity of casinos in America. As stated in the beginning of the book. This is not an effort to analyze the phenomenon of gambling or to express an opinion for or against it; the bible is already clear on this activity. I seek only to relate this information as a means of illuminating how seriously Christian ministries have drifted toward similar activity.

    In our great country of America, we protest many things. The church community surely has its causes, from abortion to pornography and many other things. Several years ago, the idea of casinos began to emerge as a way to offset the economic problems and monetary crises experienced by states and localities across the country. Thus, the growth of the casino industry became the prevailing issue of the time. Obviously, this became a cause for the Christian community, and rightly so. The breakdown in the moral fabric of the community and the promotion of greater poverty were just two concerns.

    Gaming outlets are about 1,500 strong on the mainland and over 2,000 online and all of them function according to what they purpose themselves to be. No one has to wonder or engage in some investigative exercise to determine what they are. They are a part of the world's culture and are out front with a mission that promotes the same. We spend a lot of time and fuss about what the world is doing, and perhaps that is a legitimate use of energy at times. But the truth is that the world will be the world and that is not going to change until Jesus comes. What is not expected and should be chiefly a concern of ours is that the church is increasingly taking on the image of the world. This is completely adverse to the admonition of the Apostle Paul in Romans 12:2, "…and be not conformed to this world but be transformed by the renewing of your mind*"*. The reason we have to have a renewed mind, "…that ye may prove what is that good, and acceptable, and perfect will of God."

Matthew 16:18 says, "And I say also unto thee, that thou art Peter, and upon this rock I will build my church; and the gates of hell shall not prevail against it." Simon is represented as the rock on which Christ's church is built. Jesus has given to the church the keys to the kingdom. What authority it is and what great responsibility we possess. Though this passage has been interpreted in various ways, it certainly cannot be denied that it suggests that there is a tremendous charge placed upon believers to affect change in this dark and perverse world. The word *church* is translated in this passage *ecclesia* which means separated or called out. We are the separated, *the called out* of God, to go into the world and make a distinguishable change. Indeed, we are the Lord's ambassadors, his representatives. We have been given stewardship of the gospel message, to take the Good News of Christ to the ends of the earth. The calling is so great that no one can actually enter the kingdom of heaven without us providing them the way. Jesus is not here in the flesh any longer but he has left us here to do his business. Paul, in that famous passage, makes the case:

> "If thou would confess with thou mouth the Lord Jesus, and believe in thine heart that God hath raised him from the dead, thou shall be saved… For whosoever shall call upon the name of the Lord shall be saved. How then shall they call on him in whom they have not believed? and how then shall they believe in him in whom they have not heard? and how can they hear without a preacher? And how can he preach except he be sent…" Romans 10:9-15

Paul is really saying that one who seeks to call upon the name of the Lord with the intent of getting saved has to first believe in him. If one will have the opportunity to believe in him, one has to hear about him. Furthermore, how can one hear about him except the gospel is shared? Well, it seems to me that since we are the only people on earth that God has entrusted with the gospel, if we choose not to share it or share it in an erroneous way, men, women and children will be lost.

In Acts 8 there is a beautiful picture painted by the physician Luke that speaks of our great challenge of handling the gospel message in a proper manner. There is a eunuch who had come down from Jerusalem to Gaza who traveled that desert road for the purpose of worshipping. On his return back home the Holy Spirit moved upon Philip, the evangelist, to go and join with the chariot that this eunuch just happened to be riding in. What was he doing? He was reading a passage of scripture that was taken out of the 53rd chapter of the book of Isaiah. He was reading but he did not understand. When Philip joined with the eunuch, he raised a question, "Do you understand what you are reading?" The eunuch responded by saying, "How can I understand except someone should guide me."

What a great opportunity placed upon Philip at that moment as the eunuch responded to his question. Would Philip take advantage of this opportunity to share the riches of the gospel of Christ with this Ethiopian eunuch? Would he take advantage of the man that he might gain the material riches from him in return for the gospel that he had to share? The evidence is very clear. Philip lifted himself up into the chariot, sat near the man, and began to patiently explain to him what the message of the gospel actually was. Philip, having done his job in sharing the gospel, yielded now to the convicting power of the Holy Spirit. This man was convicted and began to ask questions about the scripture that Philip had read. "Was the prophet speaking of himself or someone else?" he asked. Philip said, in substance, he speaks about Jesus. As they traveled along that road, they came to a body of water. It was here that eunuch said, "Alas there is water what hinders me now from being baptized?" Philip said, "You can be baptized if thou believe," and the eunuch said "I believe." So they both went out into the water and he was baptized and afterwards, the Holy Spirit carried Philip on to another place.

We have an awesome responsibility as stewards of the gospel message of Jesus Christ.

What All Casinos Have In Common

Attraction

Some of the most beautiful and elaborate architectural designs that you will ever see are in casinos. Tunica County, in my beloved state of Mississippi, was known nationwide as the poorest in the nation. But now, located just outside of Memphis, it is known as one of the most exciting and frequented places for gambling in the country. When one drives down Highway 61 from Clarksdale, Mississippi toward Tunica, one only has to drive a few miles before it appears that one is transitioning into a dream world. Many visitors are brought by busloads and cheap flights. A new world seems to open up with beautifully designed casinos and resorts. They are intricately and attractively designed to be luring and to make it difficult for one to resist stopping, at least to take a "peak." My first of three opportunities to visit a casino was to do a presentation on a subject that I was invited to address in a seminar.

The casino, as I remember it, was huge with two floors and many private gaming rooms. The hotel had spacious, luxurious rooms and several restaurants. The gaming area was loud and chaotic at times with all the crowds, but the total effect is one of great fun. This was just one of many casinos; others have golf courses, tennis courts, water sports areas and just about any diversion a tourist could desire. There were even supervised children's amusement areas where kids could play games and have fun with or without their parents. These places give off an air of expensive taste, plush carpet and expensive lighting, so that people will envision themselves as what they want to be, rich. Hotel rooms, food and other accommodations are kept at modest prices so as to make it affordable to most. The music, lighting and physical arrangements are psychologically engineered to control the thinking of those playing the games.

Gaming

Mark Twain shrewdly observed that *the best throw of the dice is to throw them away.* So many today no longer agree. Gambling, otherwise known as gaming or playing games of chance, is the chief focus of casinos and the newest "Great American Pastime." Baseball, has always been known as America's national past time, but is rapidly being replaced by a five hundred and fifty billion dollar a year compulsion. Gambling satisfies our MEistic, instant gratification mindset that leads us all too often to an end of ruin. How can something that is proven to bring so much atrophy be so alluring? The answer quite simply is that "it's fun" and there is the appeal of the possibility of "increase." Money is the ultimate objective, because casino gaming is sold as excitement and the ideal way to make a huge amount of effortless money in a short while. It is never advertised information about the problems that come along with the quest.

Among the underprivileged populace, you might see colleagues seduced by the promise that the lottery is the way out of a despairing situation, though the odds are hopeless. If you are employed in a casino child care center, you will inevitably witness, children being brought to be supervised while the parents are busy gambling. Beyond this, families are thrown into bankruptcy as husbands, wives, and sometimes children become addicted to casino gaming. Consequently, deep depression and many times suicide are the results. Interestingly, though we understand the possible turmoil that may come along with gaming, our actions seem to suggest ignorance on the subject. When somebody is "gaming" you, you don't think about it from a positive perspective but as a trick or an effort to get you into a place of disadvantage. Since casinos specialize in games, which so often bring about the above-mentioned consequences, why do so many willingly continue their drive toward these appealing yet serpentine localities? There can be only one reason; they feel like they can beat the game.

I remember when I started college, I was green (naïve) and wasn't "hip" to the deceptive games that many in the inner city were playing. Consequently, I got swept up in one of their crooked games. As I was walking towards the baseball field one day after class, I saw a crowd assembled in semi-circle. They were watching a rather "slick looking dude" down on his knees shuffling three shells around on a square piece of wood. I joined the crowd and watched with great glee as he shuffled the shells around with a small pea under one of the shells. After he finished each time, he'd ask the crowd, "Guess where the pea is?" and somebody would guess. If someone got it correct, ten dollars was the prize. I thought to myself "This is easy. I can beat this game." Each time, I was sure that I saw where the pea was, but when I guessed I was wrong. I thought how could I be wrong? After all I saw the pea with my own eyes. But it was years later before I understood how the game was played. It was a trick, and I was hoodwinked!

In addition to the games of chance offered such as slot, board, and card games, there are other tricks that casinos consistently use to hook people, draw them in and keep them there. Laurie Meekis in *How Casinos Lure in Gamblers and Try to Keep Them There* gives ten convincing devices that casinos use to work their magic. Her words paint a rather clear picture.

> *Casinos spend a great deal of money on little gimmicks to draw you in. Once you are there, they want to keep you there... There is lots of visual activity in a casino, to catch your eye and draw you in.*

Every machine makes some kind of sound during the play... If you are sitting there or walking by when someone wins, it gives everyone the feel that they can win too. They also have their own musical sounds, depending on what the theme to that particular machine is. When you have a whole area of the casino making happy noises, it makes the atmosphere more festive.

The slots give near wins and small wins. Seeing the big jackpot just one tiny spot away on your last spin, makes you think, "Hey I almost won. I am going to try again" or that is what they hope...Even when you lose all your money, you don't leave empty handed. ...You don't leave with a sense of total loss when you get freebies or special discounts.

The casinos know how to play on your emotions and hopes. They are experts at it. They know how to set a mood to draw you in, and keep you there. They have thought everything out very carefully.

... Colors that keep you feeling comfortable and mesmerized...This is like taking a child to the circus or toy store. Everything is shiny and bright... They make the displays appeal to every level of spending too, from people on a budget on the small change machines to the high rollers.

Exploitation

Casinos could not game and be as lucrative as they are unless they engage in exploitation of those who come. The bottom line is, they want your money and will do what they need to get it. According to Lila

Shapiro of the *Huffington Post*, people earning less than $15,000 will spend more than 20% of their income on lottery tickets. Casinos want the money and it matters not to them that you may be struggling and barely making it. They don't care that you can't pay your bills, young and trying to start a life or old and at the end of your life, money is the name of the game.

They don't ask you to fill out forms describing what your financial ability is and whether you can afford to engage in gambling. They won't ever say "we won't take your money" or "you can roll the dice free." They take money because that is what they are in business to do. Casinos will be casinos and exploitation is how they thrive. Gambling drains the economic provisions that God makes for his people. In other words, God has blessed you with a job to make money so that you will be able to make ends meet, and you have taken his provisions and used them in a place that is designed to exploit.

If you win the first time, there will not be too many more times that you will win. They won't tolerate that because it undermines their purpose for existing. Gaming's success depends on moods of despair, powerlessness and desperation. Casinos function as parasites and predators that prey primarily on the penniless. The irony is that the gaming industry perpetrates their activity. While claiming to be a positive effect on the larger community by providing revenue for education and other areas that requires funding, in reality casinos are a sophisticated shell game.

Casinos Will Be Casinos

Points of Emphasis

- Casinos are very much a part of the American society and all have commonalities that characterize their purpose for existing.

    - Lure and attraction of intricately designed and luxurious centers to peak the senses.

    - Games of Chance that the frequenters have been sold on to make them feel that they can hit it big.

    - Exploitation of the vulnerable which are those usually earning less than $15,000 per year.

Chapter III

Striking Similarities

As much as it pains me to say, there are some striking similarities between casinos and modern day ministries. There is a great hustle going on within the church community to draw the masses, not with the pure gospel of Christ but with means that look a lot like the gaming world. Like casinos, modern day ministries use techniques to lure the vulnerable in for the purpose of exploitation.

Attraction

Jeffery C. Billman, in the *Orlando Weekly,* wrote an article entitled "Viva Las Jesus" which is written from a non-Christian view. He talks about the "Wal-Martization of the Church..." and it's about excitement, flashing lights and loud drums. It's dancing in the aisles and praising Jesus until your voice goes hoarse. Obviously, there is nothing wrong with lights and excited praise. In fact, where I serve as pastor, we often get loud and turn up the enthusiasm with the best of them. It is not the cosmetics that are problematic, though they play a significant role in creating attraction. Rather, it is the dangerous message that's being heralded from pulpits, in retreats and arenas across the country. The malignant message of health, wealth and prosperity seductively siphons people in on the guise that a present day God should be used as a *slot machine ready to pay off.*

Implicit in these messages and marketing strategies is the notion that one only needs to name it by faith, sow the right financial seed and God will respond in kind. Christians are now migrating from smaller, more humble worship facilities to larger, more extravagant ones thinking that God awaits them with a breakthrough and financial increase. This "hitting it big" mentality is actually an affront to God because the assumption is that one needs to take a journey to find God. It also suggests that God can be manipulated into doing what we will for him to do. The Prophet Elijah's experiences remind us that God is not always in that which is loud and conspicuous.

"And he arose, and did eat and drink, and went in the strength of that meat forty days and forty nights unto Horeb the mount of God. And he came thither unto a cave, and lodged there: and, behold, the word of the LORD came to him, and he said unto him, What doest thou here, Elijah? And he said, I have been very jealous for the LORD God of hosts: for the children of Israel have forsaken thy covenant, thrown down thine altars, and slain thy prophets with the sword; and I, even I only, am left; and they seek my life, to take it away. And he said, Go forth, and stand upon the mount before the LORD. And, behold, the LORD passed by, and a great and strong wind rent the mountains, and brake in pieces the rocks before the LORD; but the LORD was not in the wind: and after the wind an earthquake; but the LORD was not in the earthquake: And after the earthquake a fire; but the LORD was not in the fire: and after the fire a still small voice. And it was so, when Elijah heard it, that he wrapped his face in his mantle, and went out, and stood in the entering in of the cave. And, behold, there came a voice unto him, and said, what doest thou here, Elijah?" I Kings 19:5-18

God does not need theatrics or extravagance to reveal himself. He has already done so, having created the heavens and the earth. Psalm 19:1 tells us that his creation speaks of his glory. What he wants now are committed messengers that will declare his word in an unselfish way that promotes Jesus and not us. The ministry experiences of John the Baptist were not marked by extravagance, yet according to our Lord there were none more effective.

"And as they departed, Jesus began to say unto the multitudes concerning John, What went ye out into the wilderness to see? A reed shaken with the wind? But what went ye out for to see? A man clothed in soft raiment? behold, they that wear soft clothing are in kings' houses. But what went ye out for to see? A prophet? yea, I say unto you, and more than a prophet. For this is he, of whom it is written, Behold, I send my messenger before thy face, which shall prepare thy way before thee. Verily I say unto you, Among them that are born of women there hath not risen a greater than John the Baptist: notwithstanding he that is least in the kingdom of heaven is greater than he. Matthew 11:7-14

It is evident from the above scripture that John's focus was the kingdom. When he came on the scene, he did not go to uptown Jerusalem to set up church. One would think that with his talents and being the new preacher on the scene, John would maximize that advantage by seeking out the most prime location so as to lure the crowd. No, John set up in the most unlikely of places, the wilderness. He didn't worry about bright lights or dressing in fancy clothes. When we read about him, he had an old coat made of camel's hair and ate locusts and wild honey. His effort was not to make variety in his preaching a thing of importance. He had one pet sermon he preached with the anointing of the Holy Spirit, *"Repent, for the Kingdom of Heaven is at Hand."* John just kept saying it! People came from uptown and all around to find him in the wilderness. In fact, the numbers were so great that the religious powers in Jerusalem became concerned. Interrogators came with questions. *"Are you Jeremiah?"*

"No," he said.

"Are you Elijah?"

"No," he said.

"Are you that other prophet?"

"No," John said.

"Who are you then?" they asked.

"I'm just a voice, a voice crying in the wilderness," he responded. *"Prepare ye the way of the Lord"* (John 1:21-22). Not long after that, Jesus came to visit John's little church in the wilderness requesting to be baptized. After baptizing Jesus, John received the ultimate confirmation of his message and ministry. God the Father introduced his son right there in his little church in the wilderness. Ah, what lessons ministries can learn from John today! His message was right and his motives were pure. No lights, games or gimmicks, but his sole purpose was to exalt Christ. "He it is, who's coming after me is preferred before me, whose shoe's latchet I am not worthy to unloose" (John 1:27).

Exploitation

Messengers representing Christ are sent into the field to be a blessing to people and not to exploit them for selfish gain. The scriptures are clear regarding those that Satan sends out to take advantage of the sheep through their evil deception. The casino age message of health, wealth and prosperity is a part of his deceptive arsenal.

> "Take heed therefore unto yourselves, and to all the flock, over the which the Holy Ghost hath made you overseers... For I know this, that after my departing shall grievous wolves enter in among you, not sparing the flock. Also ... shall men arise, speaking perverse things, to draw away disciples after them?" Acts 20:28-31

'Beware of false prophets, which come to you in sheep's clothing, but inwardly they are ravening wolves.' Matthew 7:15

'And Jesus answered and said unto them, Take heed that no man deceive you. For many shall come in my name, saying, I am Christ; and shall deceive many.' Matthew 24:4-5

'Now I beseech you, brethren, mark them which cause divisions and offences contrary to the doctrine which ye have learned; and avoid them. For they that are such serve not our Lord Jesus Christ, but their own belly; and by good words and fair speeches deceive the hearts of the simple.' Romans 16:17-18

"Beloved, believe not every spirit, but try the spirits whether they are of God: because many false prophets are gone out into the world." 1 John 4:1

"For when they speak great swelling words of vanity, they allure through the lusts of the flesh, through much wantonness, those that were clean escaped from them who live in error. " II Peter 2:18

"Preach the word...For the time will come when they will not endure sound doctrine; but after their own lusts shall they heap to themselves teachers, having itching ears; And they shall turn away their ears from the truth, and shall be turned unto fables. But watch thou in all things... make full proof of thy ministry." II Timothy 4:2-5

The above passages make it incontrovertibly clear that a major tactic Satan will use to throw children of the kingdom off course is erroneous doctrine. It is incumbent upon us who are messengers of God, stewards of the word, and concerned about the well being of souls, to expose this dangerous doctrine. Indeed we have an obligation to do so. Like those who perpetrate their cons and bamboozlements in the casino world, misguided handlers of the gospel look to exploit the saints in the world of Christendom. Exploitation, however, does not happen without there being fertile ground for it to germinate and come to fruition. Certain types of people are more prone to be exploited than others. **Let's consider some.**

Sign Seekers, who always look for some dramatic phenomenon to take place, are fertile ground for exploitation. Like those drawn to the bright lights and sounds of casinos expecting to hit it big, they come looking for their miracles. In a sense, it is like they are looking for God to drop a star from the sky or cause some visual manifestation to validate his authenticity as God. Oh, how often do we have the Lord right in our midst and don't recognize him! This was the mindset in Jesus' day.

> "...A wicked and adulterous generation asks for a miraculous sign! But none will be given it except the sign of the prophet Jonah... The men of Nineveh will stand up at the judgment with this generation and condemn it; for they repented at the preaching of Jonah, and now one greater than Jonah is here. The Queen of the South will rise at the judgment with this generation and condemn it; for she came from the ends of the earth to listen to Solomon's wisdom, and now one greater than Solomon is here."
> Matthew 12:38-45

In Cana where he turned the water to wine, Jesus met a certain nobleman who requested Jesus to come to his home and heal his sick child. Jesus felt it important to say, *"Except ye see signs and wonders, ye will not believe"* (John 4:48).

My belief is that these words were meant for those following him, and who were caught up in the trappings surrounding him but not really caught up in him. Sadly, the same is true today with the emphasis of ministries becoming more and more about what we can get from him as opposed to what we can do for him.

__Ignorance of the Word of God__ is also fertile ground for exploitation. Whereas with casinos, the exploitation is of those who are less educated and poor, in the arena of health, wealth and prosperity, it is ignorance of the word. When you don't have sufficient knowledge of the word of God for yourself, you are open to be manipulated by somebody else's schematic use of the word. All who handle the sacred word of our Lord are not doing so by adhering to the Apostle Paul's admonishment. Paul told Timothy to "study to show yourself approved unto God; a workman that need not to be ashamed **rightly** dividing the word of truth" (II Timothy 2:15). There is always a price to be paid for ignorance.

Winford Claiborne of *The International Gospel Hour* descanted about those who would twist a scripture to try to sustain their views of "health, wealth and prosperity" doctrine. Claiborne espouses that preachers seem not to know that some of the Lord's greatest servants, like Paul and Trophimus, were sometimes poor and sick. Paul explained to the Philippians: *"I know both how to be abased, and I know how to abound: everywhere and in all things I am instructed both to be full and to be hungry, both to abound and to suffer need"* (Philippians 4:12). If God makes all of his faithful servants rich and healthy, then neither Paul nor Trophimus was a faithful servant. Sadly, so many saints have been exploited to the point of seeming to exhibit behavior less like Paul and Trophimus and more akin to the Rich Young Ruler.

The Apostle John alludes to the importance of knowledge when he uses the word "know". This means that since it is often mentioned, it must have significance.

> *"We know that whosoever is born of God sins not; but he who is begotten of God keeps himself, and*

that wicked one does not touch him. And we know we are of God, and the whole world lies in wickedness. And we know that the Son of God has come, and has given us an understanding, that we may know him who is true, and we are in him who is true, even in his Son Jesus Christ. This is the true God, and eternal life" I John 5:18-20.

The emphasis is on the word "Know". In the original language he uses the word "oidamen" which literally means – full or complete knowledge. "My people are destroyed for lack of knowledge: because thou hast rejected knowledge," says the prophet Hosea. (Hosea 4:6) He suggests that our quality of life is inextricably tied to what we know. It is the knowledge of the word of God and his principles that we are willing to infuse into our lives on a consistent basis, which will give us a content and abundant life. It is not employing the "name it and claim it" technique as proposed by those who handle the word in error, but by being a good steward as advocated by Jesus in Matthew 25:20-21:

> *"And so he that had received five talents came and brought other five talents, saying, Lord, thou deliveredst unto me five talents: behold, I have gained beside them five talents more. His lord said unto him, "Well done, thou good and faithful servant: thou hast been faithful over a few things, I will make thee ruler over many things: enter thou into the joy of thy lord."*

Personality driven saints are also fertile ground for exploitation. I want to take the liberty of again creating a term that best describes aspects of the church today. The church of today in a sense, is suffering from what I would term, "Corinthian Churchitis." The problem of the Corinthian church can really be described by examining the first few verses of I Corinthians 1:1-2, 11:

"Paul, called to be an apostle of Jesus Christ through the will of God, and Sos'thenes our brother, Unto the church of God which is at Corinth, to them that are sanctified in Christ Jesus, called to be saints, with all that in every place call upon the name of Jesus Christ our Lord, both theirs and ours: For it hath been declared unto me of you, my brethren, by them which are of the house of Chloe, that there are contentions among you."

    The Apostle Paul really began, as he always did in his letters to the various churches, by saluting them or esteeming them for their positive attributes. In the second verse he says several things that are noteworthy. First, he calls them sanctified. Secondly, he says they are called to be saints; and thirdly, he says they call upon the name of Jesus our Lord. These three things attest to the fact that they have salvation; they are a part of the body of Christ. However, we understand that it is very possible to be saved by the precious blood of Christ and bound for heaven, but have some serious defects in other areas. The same Paul who honors them for being sanctified, saints, and having called upon the name of the Lord in verse 2, reproves them in verse 11 of the same chapter. Paul had heard that they had contentions of an elementary sort among them and proceeded to send them a written reprimand. What were the contentions that Paul cites? I Corinthians 1:12-17 gives clarity:

"Now this I say, that every one of you saith, I am of Paul; and I of Apollos; and I of Cephas; and I of Christ. Is Christ divided? was Paul crucified for you? or were ye baptized in the name of Paul? I thank God that I baptized none of you, but Crispus and Gaius; Lest any should say that I had baptized in mine own name. And I baptized also the household of Stephanas: besides, I know not whether I baptized any other. For Christ sent me not to

baptize, but to preach the gospel: not with wisdom of words, lest the cross of Christ should be made on none effect."

The problem that the Corinthian church was experiencing is not at all different from the problem that the Church of the Lord Jesus Christ is experiencing today. The Corinthian church had a problem with being personality driven. The contentions that they were experiencing were because of disputes that arose among them about a favorite preacher and who brought them into the body of Christ. Each was esteeming his or her minister above the other. They had a personality complex. I need not tell you that this expresses a great degree of carnality and immaturity, but isn't that what we see today? Today we live in an age where technology is at its pinnacle and we are able to view Christian programs from many different mediums.

Television and the Internet provide us around the clock access; we even have telephones that allow us to pull up YouTube or stream live videos at any time. All of thesem mediums can be a tremendous blessing. However, in all too many cases we have the Corinthian Church mentality, in that we have made gospel carriers into stars instead of being just messengers of the unadulterated gospel of Christ. We see them in another light, a light that is actually in competition with the light of Jesus Christ.

Consequently, because men and women have been esteemed so highly, their message carries great weight not because Christ is central, but the messenger becomes the dominant personality. Why is this so bad? If the wrong message is being perpetuated or proclaimed, those who are personality driven will take the erroneous message as truth and thereby is set on a spiritual course that is not beneficial to kingdom growth or the well being of that individual. In any message of the gospel, Christ has to be presented as the center and circumference. When Christ becomes less important than the person who speaks his name, that person has become much too large. All across the country, arenas are being filled because some famous Christian TV personality is coming to town. Obviously there is nothing fundamentally wrong with that, but if the message is not legitimate then many are led astray.

Striking Similarities

Points of Emphasis
- There are striking similarities between the functioning of casinos and the purveyors of the health, wealth and prosperity message.

- The attraction of the cosmetics surrounding ministries and the promoted prospect of hitting it big by getting a financial breakthrough of some kind. This is luring to those who are snared by this message.

- Exploitation of the vulnerable of which there are three types:
    - Those who seek signs.
    - Those ignorant of the true word of God.
    - Those who are personality driven.

Chapter IV

The Serious Business of Ministry

Ministering to God's People Is No Game

Our success in ministering to the people of God depends on our taking what we do seriously and not view it as an opportunity to fleece people as casinos do to those who frequent them. Ministry is about God's people, and God has a record of accosting those, even his chosen leaders, for mistreating his people. Moses is the greatest of the Old Testament leaders but he was not exempt from God's chastisement when it came to his people. Israel had been in slavery in Egypt for 430 years, and it was at some time near the end of those years that God began to make provisions for their deliverance. He brought together two from the tribe of Levi, Amram and Jochebed, who would have a son in the midst of a severe persecution brought on by Pharaoh, King of Egypt. It was a persecution that sought to kill all the male children born to the Hebrews. The Hebrew nation was growing too fast but the protective hand of the Almighty God shielded a particular young child, as he would be Israel's deliverer. When the child could no longer be hidden from those who would take his life, the mother left him down by the bank of the Nile River in an ark of bulrushes. Providentially, Pharaoh's daughter just happened that day to be bathing in the water when she heard the child cry. She took that child from near the river's bank, named him Moses and took him as her own. She raised that child with the help of a Hebrew woman who happened to be Moses' birth mother. **Look at God!**

For forty years, Moses would spend his life in the land of Egypt raised as an Egyptian, taught as an Egyptian, and with all the amenities that would come to a son of a Pharaoh. However, one day when Moses happened to see the mistreatment of one of his Hebrew brothers by his oppressor, and in anger murdered the Egyptian with his bare hands and buried him in the sand. Moses then became a criminal and was exiled from the land of the Egyptians. But even in Moses' flight and exile from Egypt, God was still preparing him as the deliverer of his people. God told him that he would be the one, the only one, who would go back to Egypt and bring deliverance for the people of God.

    We understand how the deliverance took place. We've all read the story of the ten plagues, ending with the plague of the death of the first-born. They left that night in a hurry and were led down to the Red Sea where they rested. There at the Red Sea, with inhibitions on both sides and Pharaoh's army approaching behind, Moses, through the power of God, lifted his rod over the Red Sea. God moved the sea from its place, and they crossed over on dry shod.

    These people, God's people, wandered in the wilderness for forty years under the leadership of Moses. Many times they were rebellious and murmured repeatedly. When God blessed them with bread, they were not satisfied. When he gave them meat, they were still not satisfied, but they were still God's people. Moses got a command from God to speak to a rock which would bring forth water. Then, an agitated, angry Moses, instead of speaking to that rock as God had said, hit the rock in anger and said to the people of God, "Come on up here you rebels and drink." It was at that point that the great Moses, the Moses who had been prepared by God as a baby to be born in persecution, raised as an Egyptian, exiled in the wilderness to spend 40 years in training as a shepherd in the land of Jethro, and sent back to Egypt to deliver them from the land of the Egyptians, discovered that he could not speak to God's people just any kind of way. Ultimately, the life of Moses ends in a conversation with God on a mountain after God had allowed him to view the Promise Land. He said to Moses, you will not go over because you disobeyed me. God took his life and brought him on to heaven.

The point that I am making through the story of Moses is that ministry is serious business, because ministry is about the people of God. Anyone who claims to be a messenger of God needs to understand the seriousness of what he is called to do. Any message to God's people has to be pure and untainted by selfish interests. The unadulterated gospel of Jesus Christ must be preached to his people and to a lost world.

Since the gospel of Christ is primarily covered in the New Testament section of the Bible, it is important to mention that the New Testament makes it emphatically clear that the gospel is not to be used as a game. With the exception of Jesus Christ himself, our Savior, the Apostle Paul is the greatest authority in the New Testament with regard to the preaching of the gospel. He not only laid his life on the line daily, he was firm in his admonitions of how the gospel should be treated. He withstood Peter when he mishandled the gospel and severely chastised the Church of Galatia when they were moved from the true principles of the gospel. An example of this is seen in how he singled out Galatia regarding their straying from what he taught them. He is the author of thirteen books in the New Testament as he was led by the Holy Spirit. After each greeting to these churches, the Apostle Paul followed with words of commendation to that church or words of encouragement. There is a significant contrast in the tone of Paul's words with twelve churches as opposed to one. The tone seems gleeful to twelve, almost as if he is really happy to be greeting them. This is not the case after his salutation to the church at Galatia. Let me just list a portion of the words that Paul used directly after the salutation in each of the books:

- Romans 1:8 First, "I thank my God through Jesus Christ for you all . . ."

- I Corinthians 1:4 "I thank my God always on your behalf . . . "
- II Corinthians 1:3 "Blessed be God, even the Father of our Lord Jesus Christ . . . "
- Ephesians 1:3 "Blessed be the God and Father of our Lord Jesus Christ . . . "
- Philippians 1:3 "I thank my God upon every remembrance of you . . . "
- Colossians 1:3 "We give thanks to God and the Father of our Lord Jesus Christ, praying always for you . . . "
- I Thessalonians 1:2 "We give thanks to God always for you all . . . "
- II Thessalonians 1:3 "We are bound to thank God always for you . . . "
- I Timothy 1:3 "As I besought thee to abide still at Ephesus . . ."
- II Timothy 1:3 "I thank God, whom I serve from my forefathers with pure conscience, that without ceasing I have remembrance of thee in my prayers night and day . . ."
- Titus 1:5 "For this cause left I thee in Crete . . ."
- Philemon 1:4 "I thank my God, making mention of thee always in my prayers . . ."

As you can see from the above list, there is one book that is left out of the group, the book of Galatians. This book is left out of the list because after Paul's greetings to the church at Galatia, his attitude is quite different. Instead of words of commendation, there are words of anger and rebuke. Why is Paul angry? He is angry because the very gospel that he preached to the Galatians is now being substituted by some new doctrine that is undermining the message of Jesus Christ among them. After Paul's greeting to the church at Galatia, he immediately rebukes them in Galatians 1:6-10

"I marvel that ye are so soon removed from
him that called you into the grace of Christ unto

another gospel: Which is not another; but there be some that trouble you, and would pervert the gospel of Christ. But though we, or an angel from heaven, preach any other gospel unto you than that which we have preached unto you, let him be accursed. As we said before, so say I now again, if any man preach any other gospel unto you than that ye have received, let him be accursed. For do I now persuade men, or God? or do I seek to please men? for if I yet pleased men, I should not be the servant of Christ."

    Paul is angry because he has gotten word that the Galatian church had drifted away from the gospel of Jesus Christ. Every born again believer and every God called preacher, teacher, messenger should be angered when the gospel, in its purest form, is under assault. Interestingly, in this same book of Galatians, the Apostle Paul rebukes the Apostle Peter and essentially calls him a hypocrite for perverting the gospel with a view that Gentiles had to undergo circumcision before they could receive salvation. (Galatians 2:11) Paul rebukes him to his face because he chose to compromise the gospel of Christ for the satisfaction of not offending some of his Jewish friends.

    The Apostle Peter stands to be blamed even more because of the fact that he knew better. In Acts 10, Peter was given a vision from the Lord about the salvation of the Gentiles. He was sent to the house of a Roman centurion to minister the gospel of Christ and when he did so, that entire house was saved and they were filled with the Holy Spirit. I'm inclined to believe that much of the perversion of the gospel today is not because of ignorance so much as it is for self gain, gratification and convenience; in short, gaming!

    In the 1950s Eric Bernes, the psychoanalyst, wrote a book entitled *The Games That People Play.* It is the foundation for a counseling strategy called Transactional Analysis. This theory of counseling espouses the idea that the human beings consistently engages in games of manipulation.

According to Bernes, we function in three ego states. Each of these ego states, according to Bernes, is used for the purpose of maneuvering people into getting what one wants. When operating from the ego state of the parent, the person essentially acts in a kind of dogmatic manner, barking out orders to people and demanding that they do exactly what they are told. When operating from the child ego state, one might choose to be a whiner and in doing so seeks to annoy a person into finally coming to their way of viewing things, thereby getting what they want. Thirdly, when one operates from the ego state of the adult, one chooses to act in a rational manner by listening, discussing or conferring with another and in that way gets what one wants. When it comes to the ministry, such games should not be played because it is not what we want that matters but what the Lord wants.

The Games That Ministries Play

Sleight

> "That we henceforth be no more children, tossed to and fro, and carried about with every wind of doctrine, by the sleight of men, and cunning craftiness, whereby they lie in wait to deceive." Ephesians 4:14

One of Merriam Webster's definitions for the word game is, "a procedure or strategy for gaining an end." In light of Webster's definition, it is clear to me that many ministries are engaged in game playing. The first type of game is called "Sleight", for two reasons. First, in the verse cited above, there is the phrase, "by the sleight of men." The verse warns of deception, which is the premise of this book. Secondly, Sleight of Hand is actually a type of cheating done in card games, often in casino Black Jack. Another word for it is *prestidigitation* (quick fingers). Some of the words that are associated with sleight of hand are deceptiveness, cleverness, cunningness, slyness and smoothness. The motivation is always deceit. Obviously, our interest is not a Black Jack game in a casino, but the deceptive antics of those who advance the message of health, wealth and prosperity in a one sided way. All too often the gospel of Christ is being handled like a deck of game cards in the hand of a deceptive dealer.

The following are examples of how this type of gaming in ministry is done.

Example 1

It is sleighting when scripture is taken out of context. One of the more popular passages used out of context is found in the gospel of Luke 6:38. It is done for the purpose of making people feel that if they give enough money, they get their desire. *"Give and it shall be given unto you; good measure, pressed down, shaken together, running over, they will pour into your lap for by your standard of measure, it will be measured to you in return"* (*New American Standard Bible*). There is almost no passage in the Bible that stands alone with the exception, perhaps of John 3:16: Every verse must be interpreted in light of its surrounding scriptures and within the context of the entire Bible. So, to understand Luke 6:38 in its complete sense, one must consider what Jesus had said just moments earlier in previous verses:

> "And turning He gazed toward His disciples, He began to say, Blessed are you who are poor, for yours is the kingdom of God. Blessed are you who hunger now, for you shall be satisfied. Blessed are you who weep now, for you shall laugh Blessed are you when men hate you, and ostracize you, and insult you, and scorn your name as evil, for the sake of the Son of Man. Be glad in that day and leap for joy, for behold, your reward is great in heaven. For in the same way their fathers used to treat the prophets. But woe to you who are rich for you are receiving your comfort in full. Woe to you who are well fed now, for you shall be hungry. Woe to you who laugh now, for you shall

mourn and weep. Woe to you when all men speak well of you, for their fathers used to treat the false prophets in the same way. But I say to you who hear, love your enemies, do good to those who hate you, Bless those who curse you, pray for those who mistreat you. Whoever hits you on the cheek, offer him the other also; and whoever takes away your coat, do not withhold your shirt from him either. Give to everyone who asks of you, and whoever takes away what is yours, do not demand it back. Treat others the same way you want them to treat you. If you love those who love you, what credit is that to you? For even sinners love those who love them. If you do good to those who do good to you, what credit is that to you? For even sinners do the same. If you lend to those from whom you expect to receive, what credit is that to you? Even sinners lend to sinners in order to receive back the same amount. But love your enemies, and do good, and lend, expecting nothing in return; and your reward will be great, and you will be sons of the Most High; for He Himself is kind to ungrateful and evil men. Be merciful, just as your Father is merciful. Do not judge, and you will not be judged; and do not condemn, and you will not be condemned; pardon, and you will be pardoned" (Luke 6:20-37).

Clearly in the previous scripture, Jesus was not promoting an investment scheme for greedy people, nor was he advocating hoarding or lustful and filthy gain. What was Jesus advocating? He was assuring those who would be obedient by sharing of their wealth in giving of themselves and resources, by lending, loving, forsaking, understanding, being unselfish, and obeying the golden rule, would have nothing to worry about. Why, because God would see to it that their every need would be met and fully supplied, far beyond what they could imagine. He would bless them in abundance. What Jesus is really calling for here is sacrificial giving. Essentially, he said that his return for our giving would be so great that it would not only supply for our needs but it would enable us to give even more. But it is a sleight to make people believe they can have running over wealth while demanding them to give money despite the fact that Jesus did not even mention money.

Example 2

Another verse that is often taken out of context is that of II Corinthians 8:9 *"For you know the grace of our Lord Jesus Christ that though he was rich, yet for your sakes he became poor, so that you through his poverty might become rich" (NIV).* Now standing alone this verse sounds really appealing for those who would desire to promote a message of health, wealth and prosperity, but when it is looked at in context, there is actually a different message being sent as shown below in II Corinthians 8:9-15:

> "For you know the grace of our Lord Jesus Christ, that though he was rich, yet for your sakes he became poor, so that you through his poverty might become rich. And here is my advice about what is best for you in this matter: last year you were the first not only to give but also to have the desire to do so. Now finish the work, so that your eager willingness to do it may be matched by your completion of it, according to your means. For if the willingness is there, the gift is acceptable according to what one has, not according to what he does not have. Our desire is not that others might be relieved while you are hard pressed, But that there might be equality. At the present time your plenty will supply what they need, so that in term their plenty will supply for what you need. Then there will be equality: As it is written: he who gathered much did not have too much, and he who gathered little did not have too little." NIV

Again it is the context that makes the difference. Many who use II Corinthians 8:9 place emphasis on receiving and hoarding as opposed to giving. The Apostle Paul is really referring to giving. Further, the Corinthians are commended for having an eagerness to give and that their giving was clearly for the work of the kingdom. In fact, in II Corinthians 8:15, hoarding is prohibited. Now, the key here is that our giving, like the Corinthians, should be driven by our love for the work of the Lord; this is not the motive that is advocated by the health, wealth and prosperity doctrine. The motivation should not be about self but the needs of other saints.

Example 3

Philippians 4:19, "But my God shall supply all your needs according to his riches in glory by Christ Jesus." Again, standing alone, this sounds wonderful to those who would perpetuate the casino like gospel according to health, wealth and prosperity, but let's consider the context.

> "I rejoice greatly in the Lord that at last you have renewed your concern for me. Indeed, you have been concerned, but you had no opportunity to show it. I am not saying this because I am in need, for I have learned to be content whatever the circumstances. I know what it is to be in need, and I know what it is to have plenty. I have learned the secret of being content in any and every situation, whether well fed or hungry, whether living in plenty or in want. I can do everything through him who gives me strength. Yet it was good of you to share in my troubles. Moreover, as you Philippians know, in the early days of your acquaintance with the gospel, when I set out from Macedonia, not one church shared with me in the matter of giving and receiving, except you only; for even when I was in Thessalonica, you sent me aid again and again when I was in need. Not that I am looking for a gift, but I am looking for what may be credited to your account. I have received full payment and

even more; I am amply supplied, now that I have received from Epaphroditus the gifts you sent. They are a fragrant offering, an acceptable sacrifice, pleasing to God. And my God will meet all your needs according to his glorious riches in Christ Jesus." (Philippians 4:10-19, NIV)

The context of Paul's writings to the church at Philippi in the previous passage is giving for ministry and not for hoarding or self gain. Philippians 4:11-13 suggests that we should strive toward contentment and be encouraged in whatever our circumstances are. Verse 14 tells us that our reliance should be totally on the God of riches as opposed to the riches of God. Just as in Paul's admonition to the church at Corinth, previously mentioned, he commends the Philippians for giving toward the work of the ministry. The key again is that this giving of the Philippian church was driven by the love for Paul and the work he was doing for the Lord as opposed to selfish motivation as proposed by the casino age message of prosperity preaching.

Word Manipulation

In the previous section I addressed the matter of scripture being misused in a kind of sleight of the hand manner, prompting financial giving by causing one's attention to be focused on the idea of gaining wealth. In the case of word manipulation, there is an overt misinterpretation of the word of God for selfish ends. It is when one skillfully uses the word of God to support an agenda that is advantageous to the manipulator. Obviously, this is ministry malpractice because it is the Lord's agenda that should be paramount. All we do in the way of teaching and preaching should be governed by Paul's words to Timothy:

> "Of these things put them in remembrance, charging them before the Lord that they strive not about words to no profit, but to the subverting of the hearers. Study to shew thyself approved unto God, a workman that needeth not to be ashamed, rightly dividing the word of truth. But shun profane

and vain babblings: for they will increase unto more ungodliness." II Timothy 2:14

Allow me to say what I feel this seasoned veteran is saying to this young novice pastor whom he'd left in Ephesus to lead the church. Paul left Timothy there to lead the church of our God and do it with sound doctrine. He wanted him to remind the people of what he had instructed about the ways of God and what he requires. Timothy could not do it properly if he did not rightly divide the word of God. Paul told Timothy in substance, do not waste time engaging in promulgating a message that will not yield the fruit of godliness because you are striving for our Lord's approval. Isn't this really what all of us desire, the Lord's approval?

Using the word in the manipulative fashion is done when we fail to use the word exegetically (proper interpretation). There are two Greek words that make this case, exegesis (interpretation) and eisegesis (misinterpretation). Exegeting happens when the declarer of the word pulls out the real meaning as opposed to eisegeting, when one reads into the word what is not actually there. Now, what would cause one to engage in exegesis on the one hand and eisegesis on the other? Well, my brothers and my sisters, it basically boils down to what the agenda is. Indeed, if it is not God's agenda that is paramount, it will become our own and consequently the word of God will suffer ruin.

Struck by the Stars

In the American culture, performing stars play a big role in setting the pattern of conduct for the rest of society. Performers from the arenas of sports, music, television, modeling, etc., all contribute significantly to what people wear, do, how they live and even what they believe. In the Christian community, the same could be said, because of the tremendous rise in the exposure of TV ministries, mega churches and conferences of various types. Leaders of ministries have become as popular and well known as any performer in the secular world. They have mass followings and many saints are unquestionably "Star Struck." This would not be a bad thing except for the fact that unfortunately, the word of God, all too often, is being mishandled, and that mishandling leads to misdirection. I've listed some direct quotes in examples that have been and are being made by some of the most popular personalities in TV ministry, which have been embraced by many as absolute truth.

For obvious reasons, the names attached to the paraphrased quotes that follow are fictitious so as to not make this about personalities. However, each of the seven examples to follow is a direct quote, and I will comment on the error of each relative to the true message of Christ.

Example 1. Madison said:

The Lord giveth and never taketh away and just because Job said bless be the name of the Lord, don't mean that he was right when he said blessed be the name, he was just being religious.

This statement was made in an effort to promote the prosperity doctrine by explaining away the circumstances of Job. It is to suggest that Job was in error when he spoke the words, "The Lord gave and the Lord hath taken away; blessed be the name of the Lord" (Job 1:21). Again, the full context is necessary. After having lost everything he had, his oxen, mules, camels, donkeys, children, Job fell to the earth and worshipped God. It was within the framework of this ambience that Job spoke these words. Instead of folding up and succumbing to satanic pressure and cursing God, he gave God the one thing that he desires from all of his children, worship. Therefore, the statement suggesting that Job was wrong is in error; there was everything right with what Job did because he was acknowledging the sovereignty of God.

Example 2. Eric said:
Your miracle is attached to what is in your pocket right now. You're trying to hold on to it but God sent me to tell you to let it go, let it go.

How ridiculous is this statement? Jesus performed 34 miracles and not one time have we seen or read where he required money for performing miracles. At Cana of Galilee he turned water into wine and there was no money required. While at Cana a royal officer, who obviously had money, met him there requesting healing for his son. However, Jesus never asked him to give money. He simply told the man to go back home to Capernaum and his son would live. On his way back, he was met by some of his servants who told him that the child was alive and well. Again no money exchanged hands. A certain leader of the synagogue named Jairus required the Lord to come to his home to see his daughter who was at the point of death. Jesus with Peter, James and John at his side, brought that child of Jairus' back to life and everyone was astounded at the miracle. Surely one would think that this leader of the synagogue would compensate Jesus for his great miracle, but he didn't because the miracles of Jesus were not for sale.

Five thousand men and their families along the shore of the Sea of Galilee got hungry one day. Jesus took a little boy's lunch, two fish and five barley loaves of bread and miraculously was able to feed them all with twelve baskets of broken pieces to spare. There were thousands there, but no record that money was given Jesus for the miracle that he performed. The problem with the statement "your miracle is in your pocket" is it implies that somehow Jesus has not done enough. The record clearly tells us that there has been a disbursement made on our behalf by Jesus for everything we need from the Lord. "Jesus paid it all; all to him I owe. Sin has left a crimson stain; he washed it white as snow" says the songwriter.

Example 3. Robert said:
God said pick up the phone right now $1,000 persons: you are going to sow the $1,000 seed. You've got to tonight. There is a miracle on that $1,000. I know what I'm talking about. He brought me here to tell you that.

It becomes problematic to advocate that the Lord is moved to action based on a certain amount of money, because it suggests that he is partial toward the amount as opposed to the need and the person's faith. What if one only had $3 but yet had the same need and the same intensity of faith and hope? Would not God, if he is granting miracles respond in kind? These are the type questions that arise when making a miracle something that money can buy.

Example 4. Continuation by Robert:
Somebody right here in television land, God said $1,000. You're sitting there saying, you know what? All I got is a $1000. If that's all you got, oh Jesus, then you've got the miracle seed in your hand.

The statement is almost laughable, taking a person's last $1,000. Well, it is not so much the suggestion of giving one's last as it is the motive for which it is requested. In fact, in Luke 21, Jesus shows us a contrast between the giving of the rich and the giving of the poor. The poor person is a widow and the story is often called the Widow's Mites. As Jesus watches them take their donations to the temple, he sees the rich man who gave a large amount and the poor woman who only had two mites to give, but she gave it from her heart. Obviously, the lesson to be learned from this story is that of motive. This destitute widow has only a few mites to her name, but she gave them selflessly and not in an effort to get something back in return. It was her way of contributing to the work of God. The comments of Jesus speak of the worth of this woman's gift that was far beyond that of the ostentatious contribution that was given by the rich man.

Example 5. Wilson said:
Give $10 and receive $1000. Give $1000 and receive $100,000. Give one house and receive 100 houses or a house worth 100 times as much. Give one airplane and receive 100 times the value of one airplane. In short Mark 10:30 is a very good deal.

It strains me to believe that the one who actually spoke these words really believed them. As we have discussed earlier, the parable of the sower found in Mark 10, is not a "deal" about money. Over and above this, the reason for our giving should never be for selfish gain, but out of love for God and to expand his kingdom here on earth. God doesn't make deals with us! A deal is a business transaction; it implies negotiating for mutual advantage. Does this sound like God? What advantage has God in making us rich? God isn't interested in making us financially rich, but he is interested in us becoming rich in character as it is developed in us by the Holy Spirit.

Example 6. Mark said:

Jesus was not poor, Jesus had a nice house. John 1:38 says that Jesus turned to those that were following him and said come with me and they said where dwelleth thou and he said come and see and Jesus took the whole crowd with him to stay in his house. That meant it was a big house.

This passage is almost quoted accurately but for the exception of three words "whole", "crowd" and "house." House is not mentioned and the whole crowd that is referred to is not a crowd at all but just two disciples, which are actually mentioned in verse 37. Had Jesus been talking about a house, it surely wouldn't take a big house to accommodate two people.

Example 7. John said:
Jesus wore fine clothes. John 19:23 says he had a seamless robe. Roman soldiers gambled for it at the foot of the cross. It was a designer original. It was valuable enough for them to want it.

Roman soldiers gambled for the clothes of many condemned criminals. Ely Wheeler author of *Wealth as Peril and Obligation: The New Testament on Possessions* and ethicist at Wesley Theological Seminary in Washington, D.C. elucidates, "It was ordinary for prisoners to be stripped naked and looted by soldiers." Wheeler also says the soldiers were gambling for the robe Herod placed on Jesus to mock him. "I'm sure that was expensive — he got it from Herod."

The previous quotes suggest the idea, as some espouse, that Jesus was rich. Was he? The suggestion that he was rich is purely speculation. What is the truth? We know that of all the places to be born, he was born in a stable and his father is the maker and creator of all things, who could have ensured that he have a more elaborate place for his birth, Luke 2:22-24. Why didn't he? Because it would have been antithetical to the message that Jesus would promote, which was that his kingdom was not of this world. We also know that his mother sacrificed turtledoves which were usually offered by poor households, Leviticus 12:2-8. Had they been rich, a greater sacrifice would have been required of them and to do otherwise would have neglected the demands of the law. The mother of Jesus burst into praise after the angel's message. "He hath put down the mighty from their seats, and exalted them of low degree. He hath filled the hungry with good things; and the rich he hath sent empty away" (Luke 1:52-53). Does this sound like the song of a rich woman? His earthly father was a carpenter, not a wealthy profession, and continued even after his birth. He said of John the Baptist, "What went ye out into the wilderness for to see? A reed shaken with the wind? But what went ye out for to see? A man clothed in soft raiment? Behold, they which are gorgeously apparelled, and live delicately, are in kings' courts" (Luke 7:24-25). Remember, John was Jesus' first cousin and forerunner. Wouldn't it be strange for the forerunner to come on the scene and announce Jesus dressed in rags and eating locust, but Jesus appears parading around in seamless robes and luxury? I could go on citing scripture that renders the contention of the rich Jesus null, void and without foundation. There is certainly no evidence anywhere that he was wealthy from his family or from traveling with his disciples.

The Serious Business of Ministry

Points of Emphasis
- Ministry involves people, more particularly the people of God, and should never be treated as a game.

- The Apostle Paul highlights the seriousness of the gospel message in his rebukes to the Galatian Church.

- Ministries often engage in games such as a king of sleight of hand, which is deceptively using the word of God to direct one's focus of giving so as to get what one wants. The use of word manipulation is to deliberately misinterpret scripture to promote the manipulator's selfish ends. II Timothy 2:14

- Much like the citizens of the American society, saints are captured by popular names of TV ministries and mega churches who frequently mishandle scripture. It is the word being spoken that should be the focus as opposed to who is speaking it.

Chapter V

Manipulation by Misuse and Misapplication
Prosperity, Increase, Faith

The most often used and misapplied words in the arena of health, wealth, and prosperity preaching are prosperity, increase, and faith. These words can really be said to be the tools that are used by the perpetuators of this erroneous doctrine to promote their cause. Prosperity is narrowly defined only to mean financial gain or materialism. Hoarding and just plain old fashioned greed have been given the new and more inviting name of increase, while faith has been changed into an instrument that is used to maneuver and manipulate God into doing whatever we want him to do, and give us whatever we desire of him. Let's now deal with the misuse of each of these words, respectively.

Prosperity
Within the doctrine of health, wealth and prosperity, greed has been substituted for prosperity. It has been redefined to make it more acceptable and embraceable within the kingdom of Christ. It is often thought that greed, as long as it is given another name such as prosperity, is good within the parameters of this teaching. Within the framework of health, wealth and prosperity, greed is taken as a virtue and believed to be the foundation of God's desire to give us what we want. Consequently, it is perfectly normal and even desirable to be consumed with the quest for riches and wealth. After all, isn't greed the American way? Well, it may be the American way but it is surely not the way of the kingdom. In John 18:36, Jesus says "My kingdom is not of this world: if my kingdom were of this world, then would my servants fight, that I should not be delivered to the Jews: but now is my

kingdom not from hence." Jesus has much more to say on this subject. One of his more pointed parables is found in Luke 12:15-34:

"… Take heed, … for a man's life consisteth not in the abundance of the things which he possesseth. … The ground of a certain rich man brought forth plentifully: … What shall I do? … I will pull down my barns, and build greater; and there will I bestow all my fruits and my goods. …But God said unto him, Thou fool, this night thy soul shall be required of thee: then whose shall those things be, which thou has provided? So is he that layeth up treasure for himself, and is not rich toward God. … Therefore I say unto you, Take no thought for your life, what ye shall eat; neither for the body, what ye shall put on. The life is more than meat, and the body is more than raiment. Consider the ravens… God feedeth them… Consider the lilies how they grow: they toil not, they spin not; and yet I say unto you, that Solomon in all his glory was not arrayed like one of these. …And seek not ye what ye shall eat, or what ye shall drink, neither be ye of doubtful mind. … and your Father knoweth that he have need of these things. But rather seek ye the kingdom of God; and all these things shall be added unto you. … Sell that ye have, and give alms; provide yourselves bags which wax not old, a treasure in the heavens that faileth not, where no thief approacheth, neither moth corrupteth. For where your treasure is, there will your heart be also."

There are several questions that this passage answers. Verse 15 answers the question, what is life really? So many have defined life by possessions and by the substance that one accumulates. Jesus, however, clearly says that one's life does not consist of the things that one has. We, who name Jesus as Savior and are of the Christian faith, understand that ultimately this life will end and that there is more to existence than what we experience here. We will exit from these mundane shores and take up residence in a place on God's celestial shores. In the words of that wonderful hymn I love, "On Jordan's stormy banks I stand and cast a wishful eye, to Canaan's fair and happy land where my possessions lie."

The sad commentary on the actions of many people is that too much time is spent busy trying to stay here and not considering that we were created for the eternal and not the temporal. Verses 16-21 answer the question of when enough living is really enough. Enough is enough when the Lord has fulfilled his promise to us, which is to meet all of our needs. When our needs are met, it is incumbent upon us to consider the needs of others, which will never happen if we are consumed with self-satisfaction. Self-consumption leaves no room for consideration for anyone beyond one's self.

Another question that begs to be answered is what type of riches really matter? A truth that cannot be denied or deviated from is, *there are some things that money cannot buy.* We may spend all of our time attaining material riches, but we will inevitably be confronted with the fact that, *in every life some rain must fall.* Problems will appear that money cannot shield us from. Crises will emerge that will not yield to money's deliverance. Death will one day usher us into the face of eternal judgment where neither money, fame nor prestige will be of benefit to us. It is when we face these realities that we will have the need for riches in another dimension. We will have the need for the wealth of God's mercy and grace and the blood of Calvary's cross. Lastly, verses 29-33 answer the question of what should our preoccupation be. Our preoccupation should be the kingdom of God and all of its righteousness and the other things needful to have an abundant life will be provided.

What then is biblical prosperity? 3 John 1:2 says, *"Beloved, I wish above all things that thou mayest prosper and be in health, even as thy soul prospereth."* Often this particular passage of scripture is misapplied to manipulate people into believing that this passage refers to material prosperity. This is absolutely not the case here. The key words in this passage are *"even as thy soul prospereth."* One does not have to be a biblical scholar to understand that though the soul does prosper, it does not prosper as a result of material riches. How then does the soul prosper? The soul is prospering when an individual is exhibiting spiritual maturity, when one's mind is being renewed after the mind of Christ and one's emotion has surrendered to temperance and self control, and when one's will has yielded to the will of Jesus Christ. When this occurs, the apostle suggests that we are prospering. Based on that equation, one really can be financially in ruins, perhaps from his own doing, but yet still prospering. The word prosperity is used many times in the Bible, Old and New Testament, but most often the word is not associated with wealth or riches. Let's examine for a moment some biblical passages that use the word prosperity in ways other than how it is defined in this modern era.

- **Abraham and His Servant**

In Genesis 24, Abraham had grown to be an old man and was well stricken in age. God had really been good to him and he was blessed in many ways. His desire at this point in his life was concerning his son Isaac, the son of the promise, and that he would marry the right woman. Abraham was living in a land that was inhabited by heathenness nations and it was his desire that Isaac would not marry a woman from that land, but rather a woman from his homeland. To ensure that this happen, Abraham called one of his servants and made him promise to go to that land from whence he came, find a woman, and bring her back to his son so that she could become his wife. The servant asked, what if I find a woman and she will not come back with me? Abraham responded, my God will send his angel and ensure that what I desire of you will come to pass. Abraham's words sound like he's saying; God is going to prosper your journey. Well, that is actually what happens because when the servant reaches Abraham's homeland, while sitting beside the well, he prays to the Lord that God will show him this woman who was to be Isaac's wife by offering him water for himself and his camels. Just as he had prayed it, it came to pass.

Genesis 24:21 says something quite interesting. When the servant saw this woman, he held his peace and wondered within himself whether God would "prosper" his journey or not. When we read the rest of Chapter 24, we know that God did prosper his journey because he took young, beautiful

Rebekah back to the land of Canaan where Abraham was dwelling at the time. Rebekah was introduced to Isaac and he fell in love with her and she became his wife. The point I am making is that prosperity is evident in this story but it has nothing to do with health or wealth. It is prosperity of a different sort. We do need prosperity, but most of the time the prosperity we need is not financial. We need God to prosper us in other areas of our lives. There are so many complexities, trials and tribulations that the life of a Christian will be inexorably riddled with, and we will need God's favor to overcome.

One of the members of the church, where I was privileged to serve as pastor, has a daughter living in the state of Minnesota who fell seriously sick, and it required her to leave home, go there, to see her through this sickness. When she got to Minnesota, she discovered that her daughter was in need of a blood transfusion, which is not something that is difficult for doctors today to handle. Technology is surely able to accommodate that type of situation and it happens all of the time in hospitals across the country. The problem was not that she could not get the blood transfusion but that she happened to be committed to a religion that was against blood transfusions, which created a different kind of dilemma. Her mother struggled to get her to take the blood but she refused. Day after day, she had to be faced with the elders and other members of that particular faith visiting the hospital as if to encourage the daughter to stand strong on her commitment not to take the blood. What a difficult situation this mother was faced with. Her testimony is that she prayed, prayed and prayed some more. After praying she was led to her daughter's bedside to say to her in a most passionate way, "you are being asked to make a sacrifice to prove your faith and your commitment to your religion. Dear heart, why would you need to make a sacrifice when it has already been made? It was done over 2,000 years ago at a place called Calvary." I want you to know that the mother's prayers were answered. Her daughter decided to take that blood and she recovered, left that hospital and went on back to her husband

and children to live and enjoy life. Again, the above situation of the story is evident that, yes, God does prosper us but sometimes, more times than often, it is in an area that has nothing to do with money. All the money in the world could not help the mother's situation. She needed God to prosper her by moving on the heart of her daughter that she would make the right decision.

- **Joseph and His Brothers**

One of the widely believed tenants of this doctrine of financial prosperity is that if one is experiencing hardship and roughness in one's life, it is because one is either unspiritual or out of the will of God. The Bible clearly rejects this and it is foolish to believe. Sometimes prosperity takes some roads that are not so smooth. Joseph was gifted by God to see the future. He is often referred to by many as the Old Testament character that was most like Jesus. He just happened to be in a family with jealous and envious brothers, because he was favored by his daddy and given, what the Bible calls "the coat of many colors." His own brothers caught Joseph one day and put him in a pit with the intent of letting him die, but God's providence and destiny brought him out. If that was not evil enough, his brothers sold him as a slave to the Ishmeelites and they took him down to the land of Egypt. That was rough treatment. But sometimes we must endure some "necessary roughness" in order to ascend to the place where God ultimately wants us to be.

While in Egypt, Joseph was the slave of Pharaoh's number one man, Potiphar. God blessed Joseph to earn the favor of Potiphar, who put him in charge of all that he owned. Essentially, Joseph had the keys to everything. He had gone from the pit to Potiphar's house, but the roughness was not over and the worst was yet to come. He was accused of attempting to rape Potiphar's wife and was put in prison. Going down, but still progressing towards God's best. He had gone from the pit to Potiphar's house and now he was in prison! When God is with you, even in prison, you have his favor. He was made trustee in the prison and eventually was sent for by Pharaoh, who heard that he could interpret dreams.

He was brought to Pharaoh and was able to relieve Pharaoh's tension and anxiety by interpreting his dreams. In response and reward, Pharaoh exalted him to something akin to Secretary of Agriculture, the second in command to the Pharaoh. He went from the pit to Potiphar's house, to prison and now to Pharaoh's palace! Now that's prosperity, but he took some rough roads to get there.

Another reason to see the fallacy in this doctrine is because the scripture teaches that prosperity can also be associated with the wicked. There is a passage in Job that makes this abundantly clear.

> "Why do the wicked live, reach old age, and grow mighty in power? Their offspring are established in their presence, and their descendants before their eyes. Their houses are safe from fear, and no rod of God is upon them. Their bull breeds without fail; their cow calves and does not miscarry. They send out their little boys like a flock, and their children dance. They sing to the tambourine and the lyre and rejoice to the sound of the pipe. They spend their days in prosperity, and in peace they go down to Sheol. They say to God, Depart from us. We do not desire the knowledge of your ways. What is the Almighty, that we should serve him? And what profit do we get if we pray to him?" *(Job 21:7-15, English Standard Version)*

The wicked in the above passage makes my case better than I am able to make it myself. The picture is of someone who has not honored God in any of his deeds but yet he seems to be prospering at least in the material way. His health is good, his children, his cattle and livestock seem to be increasing, yet there is the absence of God in his life. So he raises the question, what profit does he get from praying to God or honoring the ways of God? After all, he has all of the things that he would desire so what would he need God for? Why would we be advocating a message of prosperity that even the dope pushers and the pimps can attain? Our cause is to proclaim a gospel that sets us apart from the world and not one that patterns the world.

- **Father Knows Best**

Our God is the supreme commander of the universe; he's a provider, protector and sustainer of the entire cosmic arrangement. But the greatest role that he plays relative to his interaction with us is the role of a father. He is a father, and father knows best. If we are not disciplined in our behavior, riches and wealth could be the very thing that lures us away from him. When the father sees that there is something we are reaching for that hampers and hinders our relationship with him, he will deny us of having it because the relationship is more important. Remember that God as Father, is on a continual basis nurturing, molding and shaping us for his future purpose. He is all knowing and those things that may look immensely appeasing but have hidden harms, he shows his love by standing guard to protect us from them. Solomon, the wise king says:

> "Remove far from me falsehood and lying; give me neither poverty nor riches; feed me with the food that is needful for me, lest I be full and deny you and say who is the Lord?" (Proverbs 30:8-9, *ESV*)

Isn't this the mentality that people have when they frequent casinos day in and day out? They take their hard earned money that could best be used for bills and survival needs, and feed a slot machine or place on a table in Black Jack. They do this almost religiously believing that they will hit it big. God our Father knows what is needful for us. I am thankful that in spite of me, and what I may desire, he looks out for my best interest.

Increase

Another term that is being tossed around to support this unsound doctrine is financial increase. It is used primarily to suggest that if one would just sow the right seed, the seed being an amount of money, one can receive a financial increase. Again, this is promoted by a misuse of scripture taken out of context to support this ridiculous idea. The section in the Bible that is often used in these cases is Mark 4:1-20, where Jesus gives the famous Parable of the Sower. The parable tells of one who owns a field and went out to plant seeds in that field in an effort to bring about a harvest. The farmer sowed his seeds on varying types of ground. He sows seeds on wayside soil, stony soil and thorny soil. These three particular soils did not yield any fruit that amounted to anything worthy of the Lord's commendation. However, the sower also sowed on, what the parable terms, good ground and had the benefit of reaping a harvest. Now, it is at this point that scripture is taken out of context. Verse 8 says, *"And other fell on good ground, and did yield fruit that sprang up and increased; and brought forth, some thirty, and some sixty, and some an hundred-fold."* How many times have we heard this passage used inaccurately to suggest that if one would just have the courage to sow a certain amount of money, then one would reap in abundance? Yes thirty, sixty, even one hundred-fold. The trouble with this is that the scripture does not advocate this proposition. In fact, Jesus himself clearly lays out the purpose of the parable, and explains the symbolism of the terms sower, seed, and soil. Listen to Jesus' own words in Mark 4:14–20:

> "The sower soweth the word. And these are they by the way side, where the word is sown; but when they have heard, Satan cometh immediately, and taketh away the word that was sown in their hearts. And these are they likewise which are sown on stony ground; who, when they have heard the word, immediately receive it with gladness; And have no root in themselves, and so endure but for a time: afterward, when affliction or persecution ariseth for the word's sake, immediately they are offended. And these are they which are sown among thorns; such as hear the word, And the cares of this world, and the deceitfulness of riches, and the lusts of other things entering in, choke the word, and it becometh unfruitful. And these are they which are

sown on good ground; such as hear the word, and receive it, and bring forth fruit, some thirtyfold, some sixty, and some an hundred."

It is clear that to suggest that the seed represents money is completely antithetical to what Jesus proposes in this parable. Increase that is referred to in this parable has nothing to do with finances but everything to do with spiritual maturity. When the word takes root in the heart of any human being, it will manifest fruit. The degree to which it is allowed to take root will determine the level in which fruit are to manifest.

Financial increase is not always the blessing of God. Psalm 62:10 says, *"If riches increase, set not your heart upon them."* Over emphasis on financial increase esteems too highly a brand of teaching that espouses behavior which will make it more difficult for persons to embrace the kingdom of Christ. Why, in the name of God, would we want to perpetuate a message that at its core causes people to have a more difficult time embracing the kingdom of Christ? It makes no sense. Listen to Jesus talk about the difficulties of the rich:

> "And Jesus looked round about, and saith unto his disciples, How hardly shall they that have riches enter into the kingdom of God! And the disciples were astonished at his words. But Jesus answereth again, and saith unto them, Children, how hard is it for them that trust in riches to enter into the kingdom of God! It is easier for a camel to go through the eye of a needle, than for a rich man to enter into the kingdom of God. And they were astonished out of measure, saying among themselves, Who then can be saved? And Jesus looking upon them saith, With men it is impossible, but not with God: for with God all things are possible" (Mark 10:23-27).

The greater one's riches, the greater the possibility of being lured away into a rebellion against God!

Overemphasis on financial increase dispenses a brand of teaching that is deceitful with respect to what Christ really desires of us. Luke 14:33 says, *"So likewise, whosoever he be of you that forsaketh not all that he hath, he cannot be my disciple."* Once I heard an eloquent sermon preached entitled "The Christian's Contract." In that sermon, the preacher paints a picture of the many people who came to follow Jesus because they were caught up in the things that he could do, the miracles that he worked and the possibility of being associated with such a great teacher and wonder worker. The sermon suggested that Jesus essentially admonished them: "Before you come rushing in to join my movement, it is necessary for you to read the small print of the contract." So many people get in trouble for failure to read the small print of the contract. Homes are lost and families are destroyed because of the failure to read the small print of the contract. On this Christian journey, it is important for us to remember that the large print might say "everlasting life", but the small print says "deny yourself". The large print might say "a crown on the other side in glory" but the small print might say "no cross, no crown". We are called as carriers of the gospel of Christ to talk about, yes, the benefits of being associated with Christ but also the requirements of the sacrifice that he desires.

Over emphasis on financial increase bolsters a brand of teaching that encourages one to embrace something that might lead to self-destruction. I Timothy 6:10 says *"For the love of money is the root of all evil: which while some coveted after, they have erred from the faith, and pierced themselves through with many sorrows"*. Did not Jesus say in the Sermon on the Mount that where one's treasure is, there will his heart be also. One is set up for an awful end if his heart is given to material riches. Why? They are fleeting, and are here today and gone tomorrow. This recent financial crisis that we have experienced in America proves that it is not wise for one to be given to the pursuit of wealth. The stock market may crash and with it all of your hopes and dreams. We should be as the songwriter, "On Christ the solid rock I stand, all other ground is sinking sand. I dare not trust the sweetest frame, but wholly lean on Jesus name. On Christ the solid rock I stand. All other ground is sinking sand." When it comes to increase one must always remember that God never blesses us with anything for the sake and purpose of hoarding it for our own good. God blesses us that we might be able to bless others and thereby continue his cause on earth.

There is a beautiful story in the Old Testament that involves King David. David shows us how we ought to act and what we should do when God has blessed us with abundance. David had been hunted down across the landscape by King Saul. God had anointed David as King of Israel but had not yet allowed him to ascend to the throne. Saul was still the king. It came to pass that Saul died in battle after years of trying to destroy David because he was driven by jealousy. In II Samuel Chapter 9, it appears that God has given David rest from his enemies, all is well, and he has been given the throne of Israel. One would think that he would plan a big feast, and invite all of his friends to celebrate the fact that he had assumed the king's palace and all of Israel is in his hands. But David did something that seemed to me to be unusually gracious.

In the very first verse of Chapter 9, David raised a question, *"Is there yet any that is left of the house of Saul, that I may shew him kindness for Jonathan's sake?"* What a question that was! He wanted to know if Saul had any descendants left alive, not that he might destroy them but that he may be kind to them. David summoned one of the servants whose name was Ziba, and again raised the question, "Is there yet any that is left of the house of Saul, that I may shew kindness to him?" The servant said, "Yes there is one who is in a place called Lodebar; his name is Mephibosheth, the son of Jonathan." David demanded that he be sought, found, and brought to him. I'm sure when he was found fear gripped the soul of Mephibosheth. He knew absolutely nothing about what the king really wanted, but surely he have thought that he was being sought to be put to death as the last remaining ancestor of Saul, the king's enemy. Interestingly, Mephibosheth was lame after his babysitter fell with him when he was a child and permanently paralyzed him. I'm sure at this point Mephibosheth was trembling, but much to his surprise the king said, "I want to show you kindness. I am going to restore all that has been taken that belonged to your father, all of the land and property, and I want you to sit at meat at the king's table continually." What grace, what kindness, what unselfishness! David's act is really raised to another level when you consider the fact that there was nothing Mephibosheth could offer him. He was lame, which meant that he could not serve, could not dance to entertain the king and certainly could not go into battle to fight to defend the kingdom. But that's not David's concern. I believe without question that he felt such indebtedness to God for having shown him increase that he wanted to share the blessings of God with someone else.

Increase is not intended for the purpose of hoarding or selfishness, but to show the kindness of God to others. Did not Jesus put forth this principle in Luke 18, when he challenged a rich man to share his goods with the poor; and in Luke 12 when the ground of a rich man brought forth plenty, and did not have room to store the increase of his harvest? "I will build new barns," he said, "to hoard up all that I have, and say to my soul, eat soul, drink soul and take thine ease, for thou hast much stored up for many years." The word came, "thou fool, this night is thy soul required of thee." Obviously, he was a fool because he didn't consider the fact that God blessed him with the brightness of the sunshine, the rain and the proper climate that he might have the harvest. Having been the recipient of these blessings, it should not have been too difficult for him to be mindful that he needed to share with those who did not have what he did. The true message of the gospel is not that we seek after riches and wealth to satisfy our insatiable appetites, but to have the mind of Christ and to give unselfishly. God will then favor us with even more.

Faith

Perhaps the most flagrantly misused and manipulated word in the theater of the health, wealth and prosperity movement is that of faith. Without a doubt, faith is the one element that enables us to relate with God. There can be no relationship with him without the existence of faith. Hebrews 11:6 says, *"Without faith it is impossible to please him; for he that cometh to God must believe that he is, and that he is a rewarder of them that diligently seek him."* Yet purveyors of this erroneous doctrine constantly promote the misapplications and even the perversion of the term faith. How is this done? It is done by advocating that saints should be overly consumed with trying to get God to supply us with blessings that are solely for the purpose of satisfying the natural man. Essentially, it is encouraging the use of faith in order to be healthy, wealthy and naturally prosperous.

Clearly, there is nothing wrong with being healthy, wealthy or naturally prosperous; all of us desire it in some form. No one who is honest will tell you that they don't want to be healthy, wealthy or materially prosperous. However, the doctrine presents several problems. First of all, God is not primarily concerned with our being healthy, wealthy or naturally prosperous, the key word being primarily. It is not his number one concern. God blesses us in the area of our health, and will even at his own choosing, provide wealth for us in varying ways. God will also provide for financial prosperity, but it is not his ultimate goal for our lives. It is the inner man that God is most concerned with. God wants to develop our character, which is at the core of the inner man.

It is the character of the inner man that will most reflect what God is really like. God's desire is to take us from a carnal nature, where we are consumed with carnal or material possessions. In Philippians 3, Paul lays out what our pursuit ought to be as he reflects on his own life. He wrote to the Philippian church, that he would not brag about his credentials of the flesh, though he could if he chose to do so. That which he in his early life would have thought to be valuable, he finds to be worthless in his new life in Christ. In verse 8, *"Yea doubtless, and I count all things but loss for the excellency of the knowledge of Christ Jesus my Lord: for whom I have suffered the loss of all things, and do count them but dung, that I may win Christ."* Further he says in verse 10, *"That I may know him, and the power of his resurrection, and the fellowship of his sufferings, being made conformable unto his death."* Paul's pursuit was to know Jesus and to be conformed into his likeness. This means the development of character, the inner man.

Again, Paul in his writing to the church at Ephesus alludes to the fact that the will of God is for us to develop the character of the inner man. Listen to the words of the apostle in Ephesians 3:14-16; *"For this cause I bow my knees unto the Father of our Lord Jesus Christ, Of whom the whole family in heaven and earth is named, That he would grant you, according to the riches of his glory, to be strengthened with might by his Spirit in the inner man."* Reading further in that chapter, the apostle says that his desire is for us to comprehend the breadth, length, depth and height of the love of Christ, which passes knowledge and that we might have the fullness of God. This is spiritual maturity and it cannot happen if our pursuit is only after that which satisfies the flesh. The other problem of advocating a use of faith exclusively for the purpose of the satisfaction of the outer man is that ultimately the outer man will cease to exist. It is the inner man that will live forever. The Bible teaches us in II Corinthians 5, that this earthly body of ours is decaying daily and ultimately will cease to exist. It just makes sense to me that since we know that our outer man is decaying and going back to the dust from whence it came, and our inner man, will one day be in eternity with God, that this should be our primary focus.

Another fallacy presented by this Casino Age perspective of the gospel is that it suggests indirectly, that if one is experiencing hardship of some kind, he or she cannot be walking by faith. The suggestion is that if faith is applied properly there should be no need for one to experience roughness in one's life. This is completely antithetical to what the Bible teaches. There is no clearer rejection of this fallacy than what is presented in Hebrews 11, which is called the *Faith Hall of Fame.* The writer of Hebrews presents a glorious picture of the patriarchs and their faith walks with the Lord, which led to actions that moved the heart of God. It is a picture of God's best. He takes us all the way back and tells us about Abel, Enoch, Noah, and of course, Abraham, Moses and others. But what is interesting, for the purpose of our argument, is what is said at the end of the chapter that contain the Faith Hall of Fame. The writer tells us what these great stalwarts and servants of God had to endure as a result of their faith. Some endured raging fires, many were tortured and beaten with whips, some were chained in jail, and still others were stoned to death. They were poor and in many instances, wondered in deserts and mountainous terrains, in caves and holes in the ground. They all pleased God because of their faith, but died without receiving what had been promised. It is as if the writer does not want to leave us with the impression that they lived without struggle and adversity. Their faith did not enable them to live a life like the one being presented by those who advocate the health, wealth and prosperity doctrine. Again, faith is not an instrument to be used to manipulate God into what we want him to do. Faith is confidence in a sovereign God and trusting him for his will for our lives.

Closely akin to this matter of manipulating the word faith is also the misuse of the word favor. Favor is a term that is most often used to suggest that God is smiling on us because he is showering down upon us great blessings of the kind that all of us would like to have. However, the favor of God should be considered from a much broader perspective. Because God's favor inexorably refers to actions that he performs toward us, it has to be understood in view of God's Omniscient attribute. Because he knows what's ahead and has a plan for what he ultimately wants us to become in the future, his acts of favor are a part of helping to work his will to meet that end. This means that not all he allows in our lives will we be thrilled with. In fact, it could very well be that God is showing favor to us even though we are experiencing momentary situations of unease and discomfort. This is something that is manifested throughout the word of God.

Jesus was in flight from his enemies in John 9, when he saw a man who was blind from birth. In verse 2, His disciples said to him, *"Master, who did sin, this man, or his parents, that he was born blind?"* But Jesus answered in verse 3, *"Neither hath this man sinned, nor his parents: but that the works of God should be made manifest in him."* The *New Living Translation* said that it happened so the power of God could be seen in him. Verse 4 explained, *"I must work the works of him that sent me, while it is day: the night cometh, when no man can work."* Jesus then spat on the ground and made spittle of mud, rubbed it in the man's eyes, told him to go wash in the pool of Siloam to receive his sight. That man was then able to see. Why was this particular miracle important? I believe it was for the purpose of showing those who were on-looking that Jesus was indeed the Anointed One. Consequently, a sovereign God, who knew Jesus would be at that place, at that particular time, controlled the dynamics of this event to affirm the authenticity of the Messiah to the surrounding crowd. This blind man was blessed with the opportunity to be involved in the providential work of God. I know that this does not look like favor, but anytime God uses us to show his glory and his use of power, he is favoring us. He is doing something special with our lives, and isn't that in the final analysis what it's all about? It is all about yielding ourselves to be used by him for his purpose, plan and power. Favor does not always feel like favor, but it is favor just the same.

In the famous section of II Corinthians 12 where Paul tells us about his struggle with a thorn in the flesh, we again see the favor of God working in an atypical way. Though we don't know particularly what the thorn Paul struggled with actually was, we do know that he consulted God on three occasions that God would move it from his life. This series of prayers is often presented as if he prayed in singular fashion three times, but I believe this refers to three periods for which Paul engaged in prayer. I believe that he prayed consistently and continually on three different occasions that he would be delivered from this malady. It was not until the third season that he actually found that it was not in God's will that it be moved. There were two major reasons for God's response to Paul; on the one hand, he didn't want him to get lifted in pride for revelations that he had given uniquely to Paul. On the other hand, God wanted Paul to come to a greater comprehension of his grace in times of weakness. God helped Paul to see that during weakness, one's strength through faith is most prevalent. In the words of Paul himself in II Corinthians 12:10, *"Therefore I take pleasure in infirmities, in reproaches, in necessities, in persecutions, in distresses for Christ's sake: for when I am weak, then am I strong."* I believe it is fair to say that Paul would not have spoken so convincingly in verse 10 had he not had the experience with the thorn. I'm sure it was painful, distracting, disturbing and caused him much consternation, but it was God's divine favor on his life to bring him to a level of maturity through the sufficiency of his grace. No one who has any understanding of the life and ministry of the Apostle Paul would even remotely suggest that he was not a man of faith or that he did not exercise that faith all through his life and ministry. Here though, Paul merely prays and asks the Lord for the removal of the thorn but he's not using his faith to name or claim anything in an effort to impel God to act outside of his will. Paul exhibits faith in his Lord's wisdom to know what was best for his life.

Manipulation by Misuse and Misapplication
Prosperity, Increase, Faith

Points of Emphasis
- Prosperity is narrowly defined to only refer to financial and material gain. Greed and hoarding has become a substitute for prosperity. Bible prosperity has less to do with materialism and more to do with being in the will of God.

- Increase is defined by some without the consideration that all increase is not the blessing of God. It is deceptively overemphasized. Psalm 62:10

    - It skirts around the serious demands that Christ has on our lives and encourages a lifestyle that could put one on the path of destruction.   II Timothy 6:10

    - Increase is God's way of positioning us to bless others. Luke 12

- Faith is the most overly used and misapplied word in the arena of health, wealth and prosperity.

    - Faith is not something to be used to try and get God to do what we want him to do in satisfaction of our natural being. Many men and women of faith endure hardships and never were materially wealthy. The Hall of Faith of Hebrew 11 is a considerable list of giants of the Faith.

Chapter VI
Stolen Identity

As most people in American society today, I am wired to the Internet and have a couple of email accounts. Sometimes when I check my mail I cannot help but laugh at some of the things that I happen to read occasionally. I'm sure you have been the recipient of mail from persons in Europe or Nigeria suggesting that you have inherited a large amount of money, or that you have been sent in some type of transport service, a large amount of money. Here is just a portion of one email that I recently received:

ATM International Credit
Office of the Director of Operations
Office of the Presidency
Oceanic Bank (PLC of Nigeria)

ATTN: Honorable Beneficiary

This is to officially inform you that we have verified your inheritance style and found out that why you have not received your payment, is because you have not fulfilled your obligations given to you in respect of your inheritance. You will receive your ATM card to withdraw funds from the ATM machine. However in order to obtain your card, submit your full name, address, phone number, fax number, age and a copy of your identification.

Without revealing anymore, I'm sure you know what's going on here. Yes, it is a scheme to steal my identity. Furthermore, they didn't even use correct punctuation or sentence structure. All over America and the world even, millions of people are being sucked into similar schemes for the purpose of identity theft. Some people have lost their retirement, savings accounts--even their homes. Others have had their credit records ruined because they are among those who have yielded themselves over into the hands of thieves who stole their identity. Once upon a time my wife came to me and asked if I had checked out a book at a certain library here in Jackson, Mississippi. My answer was no. She said someone had because I received a bill from the public library system saying that I had not returned a book. She then called the library system and squared that issue away with them, but much to our surprise, that was only the tip of the iceberg. Later on, she began to receive bills from department stores in the area indicating that she had made certain purchases by credit and had not paid the bills. When she looked further into the situation, she found out that she had been the victim of identity theft. It was a long and tedious process that she had to endure to get the matter corrected, but she finally did. We then took measures to ensure that it would never happen again.

Perhaps it is reaching a bit far but it is my belief that our Savior and Lord is a victim of identity theft. There are those who have hijacked his name and on a consistent basis, attaching it to behavior that he has not advocated. Several years ago, I preached a sermon entitled, "Is It Still the Lord's House?" I know it may sound like a ridiculous question given that the Bible clearly tells us that the earth is the Lord's and everything in it. Jesus also said in Matthew 16, "upon this rock I will build my church." However, based on what I have observed in messages from evangelical ministries and pulpits on television, I am inclined to believe that there is confusion regarding the ownership of the Lord's church. The gospel that he has commanded us to preach has been substituted with something that does not mirror him at all. It is akin to identity theft. One who has stolen your identify does not look or sound like you at all. However, he has taken your personal information and used it as if he is you. II Corinthians 5:20 (*ESV*) says, "Therefore we are ambassadors for Christ. God making his appeal through us . . ." An ambassador is one who acts on behalf or represents another authority. We have located in the city of New York what is called the United Nations, a place where representatives from all of the countries across the world meet and confer about various issues. The representatives are called ambassadors and each represents his own country. They do not have their own agenda but rather they are acting on the agenda of the country that sent them to be representatives. If indeed a representative chooses to take it upon himself to have his own agenda, that person becomes a renegade and can no longer be trusted by that government. Whatever the policy of that particular nation is, that ambassador is to advocate for and on behalf of that particular policy.

Well, in a similar sense those of us who have been called to preach the gospel of Christ are ambassadors for him and his representatives. We act based on and through his authority and carry his name. We do not have our own gospel nor should we have our own agenda. When we take it upon ourselves to do our own thing then we have become a renegade preacher, teacher, missionary or messenger. A preacher, who claims to be a messenger of Christ and yet promotes a message adverse to the one that Christ himself taught, cannot have the sanctioning of Christ. Promoting this message will ensure that they won't have the benefit of four important graces that the true gospel gives.

Provisions

If we are operating as an identity thief, we cannot have the *provisions* associated with carrying the true gospel. Jesus sends out a group of seventy persons two by two into the villages to preach the gospel.

> "After this the Lord appointed seventy-two others and sent them on ahead of him, two by two, into every town and place where he himself was about to go. And he said to them, the harvest is plentiful, but the laborers are few. Therefore pray earnestly to the Lord of the harvest to send out laborers into his harvest. Go your way; behold, I am sending you out

> as lambs in the midst of wolves. Carry no moneybag, no knapsack, no sandals, and greet no one on the road" (Luke 10:1-4).

These four verses make a few things clear. First of all, the harvest belongs to the Lord, which means that we are laborers in his field. The field, of course, represents the world where people he created live; all of it belongs to him, and does not belong to us. We are working for him. It pays occasionally to remind ourselves that we own nothing. Because the people belong to him, we are accountable to him for what we do as it relates to them. If we harm them, God cannot be pleased. Secondly, we are sent into the harvest by him and are not self sent; which means that what we do has to be according to his agenda and not our own. Thirdly, we have his provisions. He says carry nothing, no moneybag, knapsack, or sandals. Carry no provisions of your own and don't worry. Why would God make such an incredible demand? The answer is that he will make sure we will be provided for. Those, to whom we minister, will be moved to share of their own resources. He does not want us to be overly consumed with striving for provisions. Jesus makes it crystal clear that this will be his concern.

Peace

If we are operating as an identity thief, we cannot have the *peace* that the gospel of Christ affords.

> "Whatever house you enter, first say, Peace be to this house! And if a son of peace is there, your peace will rest upon him. But if not, it will return to you. And remain in the same house, eating and drinking what they provide, for the laborer deserves his wages. Do not go from house to house" (Luke 10:5-7, English Standard Version).

The Lord clearly says here that he gives us the blessing of having his peace and also the ability to grant his peace to others. This is a tremendous privilege to have. How sad it would be for us to strive with great effort in ministry, preaching, traveling and doing the work but at the end of the day we don't have his peace. We cannot have his peace if we are working our own agenda.

Power

If we are operating as an identity thief, we cannot have the *privilege of his power*. The most important and among the last words uttered by Jesus before he left planet earth was termed "The Great Commission."

> "All authority in heaven and on earth has been given to me. Go therefore and make disciples of all nations, baptizing them in the name of the Father and of the Son and of the Holy Spirit, teaching them to observe all that I have commanded you . . ." (Matthew 28:18-20).

The first thing that Jesus utters to them when he meets them after his resurrection were words to let them know that he was the ultimate authority, saying, "All Power." A great preacher once said, "All just means all." There is nothing above all, under all, beside all, or in front of all. After making that declaration about his power, the next word he uses is "go" as if to say, go in my power, go in my authority. When we have the privilege of his power (authority) that gives us the right to act on his behalf and are assured that he is pleased because he has sanctioned what you are doing.

Presence

If we are operating as an identity thief, we cannot have the *privilege of his presence*.

The Great Commission further states in Matthew 28:20, "Teaching them to observe all things whatsoever I have commanded you: and, lo, I am with you alway, even unto the end of the world. Amen." Christ says, "Lo, I am with you always." This means, be certain that I am there with you. In the words of this modern vernacular, Jesus is saying I've got your back. It is comforting to know that he is with us given that he's sending us among wolves. We have his presence! This was important for the disciples to hear because they also heard him say as recorded in John 14, that he was going to be leaving them. Their hearts were tremendously heavy. Such a great teacher, miracle worker, and great lover of their souls, was leaving. This had to be a tremendous thing for them to contemplate. But now, even as he is getting ready to leave, he assures them they would have his presence, not just momentarily but always, even to the end of this present age. Oh my brothers and sisters, what wonderful words these are. I have been doing this ministry for over twenty-five years, and I have had life's ups and quite a few downs. There have been some valley situations, but like David, when in the valley it has always comforted me to know that he was with me.

  The seriousness of this matter of identity theft can best be understood when we consider the two primary things that are accomplished as a result of it: (1) On the one hand, someone who steals another's identity is able to benefit by using that person's true and established credibility to advance himself through the purchase of merchandise and services for which he does not qualify. One who has worked hard to establish good credit with commercial institutions is robbed of the freedom of the use of his own credibility because it has been stolen; and (2) On the other hand, the one on whom this act has been perpetrated is severely damaged with regard to the perception that others will have of him.

  The capitalistic system is based to a large degree on credit, and one's ability to purchase an item on credit will depend on the available record of one's past performance. In fact, one's credit score will generally determine one's ability to purchasing availability. One's word does not really matter, but it is what the established record has to say, and that record could be severely tarnished if one's identity has been stolen and misused. This is exactly the case in church or religious matters when it comes to the distortion and the erroneous teachings that are perpetrated by those who would advance the health, wealth and prosperity doctrine. Essentially, what happens is that those who advance the doctrine are in many ways advantaged because they are on the receiving end of large sums of money that comes by way of offerings and or "seed sowing." However, one who ministers the word is worthy to be supported financially by those to whom they minister. This principle is biblical and should be practiced by the people of God. Paul says, "if we have sown unto you spiritual things, is it a great thing if we shall reap your carnal things?" (I Corinthians 9:11) The excesses that take place and the use of God's word in a manipulative and spurious way to satisfy selfish monetary gains are unacceptable.

Perception is another matter that we should be concerned about within the Christian arena. It is how people perceive us that can determine how effective we are in our witness to them. Because the name of Christ has been taken and used to support acts of greed, covetousness and self-gain, it has severely affected how people view the Christian church, even Christ himself. There has been a grotesque distortion of what the ministry of Christ truly is and what his mission is for those whom he left here to be his witnesses. Those of us who are clear on the message and the mission should not be hesitant in setting the record straight. In fact we are obliged to do so and ultimately will have to give an account of our stewardship of the gospel we preach and the message that is being perpetuated in Christian arenas across the country. Silence can be sinful. We are admonished to hear the words of the prophet Isaiah:

> "His watchmen are blind: they are all ignorant, they are all dumb dogs, they cannot bark; sleeping, lying down, loving to slumber. Yea, they are greedy dogs which can never have enough, and they are shepherds that cannot understand: they all look to their own way, every one for his gain, from his quarter" (Isaiah 56: 10-11).

Well, that is truly the state of the church in some instances today. There is danger approaching and we fail to sound an alarm so that those who are weak and vulnerable may be able to recognize the schemes of the enemy to deceive the people of God. What's even sadder, in my estimation, many of the perpetrators are not ignorant of the true message, but have a rapacious appetite to satisfy the flesh. Because of this, they have chosen to embrace the false message of health, wealth and prosperity because it feeds that hunger.

Let the Whole Truth Be Told

While attending a convention several years ago, it was mine to hear one of the best sermons that I have heard in my life. It was entitled, *"Let the Whole Truth Be Told."* Dr. William J. Shaw, who ultimately would become the National Baptist Convention's president, preached this sermon and used to support his points the lies that were told by the enemies of Jesus even as he hung there on the cross. He took his time and listed each one of the lies that were told on that grim day at Calvary. In Matthew 27:39-49 there are recorded several untruths and mischaracterizations of the words of Jesus.

> "And they that passed by reviled him, wagging their heads, and saying, Thou that destroyest the temple, and buildest it in three days, save thyself. If thou be the Son of God, come down from the cross" (Matthew 27:39-40).

Of course, we who know what the scriptures say and what they mean understand that what Jesus was speaking of was actually his own body. The chief priest, the scribes and the elders also got in on the conversation when they said, "He saved others: himself he cannot save. If he be the king of Israel, let him now come down from the cross, and we will believe him" (Matthew 27:42). What a huge lie that was. Had Jesus wanted to save himself, he could have done so, but his concern at this point in his ministry was not to prove anything to them, but to do the will of His Father that sent him. Thank God he chose the latter. Further it is recorded in verse 43, "He trusted in God; let him deliver him now, if he will have him: for he said, I am the Son of God." The statement here suggests that he was a phony because he said that he trusted in God and was the son of God. We know with certainty that he was and is the Son of God. These are just two or three instances where those who were his enemies mischaracterized the ministry and words of Jesus.

The lies and mischaracterizations did not stop at Calvary because when the Lord had risen as he said he would, those who were concerned about losing their influence and authority with the masses conspired. They coerced the Roman soldiers and paid them to say that the disciples stole the body lest the real story spreads. It didn't work! Jesus did die, was buried in a borrowed tomb, and was raised the third day morning by his father from on high. This is the real truth and this truth of the gospel message has to continually be told. The health, wealth and prosperity doctrine actually mischaracterizes the ministry of Jesus and what his mission and mandate for the church is all about. Indeed, the fundamental principles that Christ expects us to embrace are being undermined and short circuited by a false message that focuses on the temporal as opposed to the timeless and the earthly as opposed to the eternal.

What is the whole truth about the message of Jesus Christ? Before I begin addressing this question it should be stated that as Christians we have but one supreme perfect example and that is in the person of Jesus Christ. It is he who laid down the pattern for our lives and conduct with regard to our message and ministry. In the words of the Apostle Peter:

> "For even hereunto, were ye called: because Christ also suffered for us, leaving us an example, that ye should follow his steps: Who did no sin, neither was guile found in his mouth: who, when he was reviled, reviled not again; when he suffered, he threatened not; but committed himself to him that judgeth righteously: Who his own self bare our sins in his own body on the tree, that we, being dead to sins, should live unto righteousness: by whose stripes ye were healed" (I Peter 2:21-24).

The Apostle Paul states in his letter to the church at Corinth, *Be ye followers of me, even as I also am of Christ.* (I Corinthians 11:1) If one wants a clear picture of the life of

Jesus and how his message is characterized, it is best to check the record of the gospel writers: Matthew, Mark, Luke and John. Under the anointing of the Holy Spirit, these four writers give us a depiction of the activity of Jesus while here on earth. These writers wrote from their own perspective and sometimes give different versions of what is captured in a particular story surrounding Jesus. Though their versions of particular situations involving Jesus may somewhat differ, there is no confusion, conflict or contradiction relative to the character of Christ and what his overall message is intended to proclaim. Let's consider in the following chapter several elements that depict the message of our Savior.

Stolen Identity
Points of Emphasis
- Christ has become a victim of identity theft.

- As ambassadors of Christ we should always represent his agenda. We carry his name and represent his identity to others.

- Those who choose to promote a message adverse to Christ's will not have the provisions, peace, power and presence of the Lord that the gospel ensures.

Chapter VII
The Character of the Message of Christ

The Message of Christ is characterized by Service

As Christians, we like others of the world will function in many capacities. We will achieve many things as we navigate the various highways of life. Success is bound to come to Christians as it does to others and indeed should be expected of those who follow Christ. After all we have him living in us to help us achieve. However, it matters not what we obtain as we journey through life, we will never be able to grow beyond the requirement of being a servant. As a citizen of the kingdom of Christ, it is required of us to serve. In Mark 10, we read about the amazing dialogue Jesus had with the two sons of Zebedee, James and John, regarding their request to be his first and second in command. The complete thrust of this story is minimized if one fails to read verses 32, 33, and 34 just prior to the request of James and John. These verses lay the foundation for this enormously powerful episode involving Jesus and his disciples.

> *"And they were in the way going up to Jerusalem; and Jesus went before them: and they were amazed; and as they followed, they were afraid. And He took again the twelve, and began to tell them what things should happen unto him, Saying, Behold, we go up to Jerusalem; and the Son of man shall be delivered unto the chief priests, and unto the scribes; and they shall condemn him to death, and shall deliver him to the Gentiles: And they shall mock him, and shall scourge him, and shall spit upon him, and shall kill him: and the third day he shall rise again" (Mark 10:32-34).*

Do you get the picture in your mind? Jesus is traveling with his closest followers, his friends even. These are men who he had invested a lot of time in and had shared his most intimate thoughts. They had a close relationship. He pulled them aside and began to tell them about some awful things that would happen to him when he gets to Jerusalem. Let's look again at what he says in my words: "Fellows, it's going to be real bad for me when we get to Jerusalem. They are going to deliver me into the hands of my religious enemies, the chief priest and scribes, and they are going to sentence me to death. Then, they are going to hand me over to the hands of my Gentile enemies. They are going to make fun of me, whip me, spit on me - and guys, they are going to kill me." Now it doesn't get any more serious than this. When your closest friend comes to you and says I am about to be killed, it should put you into a certain mindset. In fact, you would want to know whether he is serious. You would want to know further into what he was talking about, and how you could help in preventing it from happening.

James and John gave a most unusual response to what Jesus had just said. Instead of being encouraging, supporting or even angry at the thought of someone handling their master in the way he described, they chose a mode of response that was completely out of left field. After hearing the grave words of Jesus, James and John said to him in verse 35, *We would that thou shouldest do for us whatsoever we shall desire.* In short, "Do us a favor." Jesus said in substance, *well what do you want me to do?* In today's vernacular they answered, "Hook us up." *When you get your kingdom started, we want you to put us on your right and left side. We want to be seated right next to you.*

The obvious question to be asked here is why did James and John make such a request at such a grave and critical moment in their journey with Jesus? I believe there were primarily three reasons for their request. First of all like many of us, James and John were more concerned about a *seat* as opposed to service. You see, James and John, like the others of that day who followed Jesus, actually were of the mindset that the kingdom of Jesus would be immediately set up with the overthrow of the Roman Empire. Therefore James and John in a sense were putting in their bid for an important job in government. It could also be assumed that since there was evidence that these two brothers were cousins to Jesus, they may have been suggesting that they ought to keep the best jobs in the family. What they were really looking for was power and prestige that came along with the seat of the position. They did not ask to be servants because in their minds, a servant was to be scoffed at and not to be honored.

Much of the dynamics that surround this matter of prosperity preaching is similar to what is happening in the text with James and John. It is a quest for power and status. On the one hand there are those who are not willing to trust God for his provisions, and that he will see to it that their needs are met. This inability to trust God leads to a "get rich quick" answer and consequently, creates subjects for those who will perpetuate a false remedy for their fix. It is the type of condition that increases the number of people at casinos.

On the other hand, there are those who arrogantly misrepresent the gospel of Christ in their pursuit of being the largest and most popular ministry on the planet. The problem with being a seat seeker is that it inevitably will cause you to do some ungodly things. It was the motivation behind King Herod to find the baby Jesus, obviously to do him harm because he had a concern about his seat being undermined. In the Old Testament, King Saul was so driven by his fear for losing his seat that he tried to assassinate King David and pursued him across the landscape like a wild animal. God is not interested in what seat you occupy; he is interested in how you serve.

I believe that another motivation behind the request of James and John was that they were more concerned about being **seen** than they were about serving. James and John saw in occupying the seat (getting the job) that they would be more visible because of a larger spotlight. They wanted the fame of being associated in such a close capacity to one whom they perceived to be the king albeit, they were thinking of an earthly king. Dr. Martin Luther King, Jr. used this famous text in his last sermon before his death, which he entitled "The Drum Major Instinct." In that sermon, Dr. King talked about the innate desire in all of us to be out front and to lead the parade (drum majors, if you will). Toward the end of that sermon, he talked about how he would like to be remembered at his funeral. He said he didn't want to be acclaimed for having won so many awards and for all the credentials and accolades that he had received over his life, but simply wanted to be remembered as one who tried to help somebody, who tried to love somebody and who tried to serve humanity. In the final analysis, it is not that we were seen of others that matter to the Lord, rather it is our service to others. In fact, Jesus pointed out in the Sermon on the Mount, "Whatever you do, should not be done with the sound of a trumpet to announce it to be seen of men, but in secret." The Lord, who sees in secret, shall reward us openly.

The final reason that I feel James and John were motivated to take this position was that they were more concerned about **self** than they were about serving. We all know that Jesus chose twelve disciples to follow him and never put one above the other. Essentially, what these two disciples were exhibiting was selfishness. How presumptuous of them to believe that they would be given these two seats beside Jesus and not the others. Why did they feel that they were so special? Well, when we become self consumed, we can never really see the concerns or interests of others, but it is completely about ourselves. Why would they have not considered Andrew? After all he was the first disciple. No! The only motivation for them was self-satisfaction.

Dr. King made another profound point in that memorable sermon about the importance of being first. One would have thought that Jesus would have condemned them, but he did not. In fact, he says it is alright to be first or even out front, as long as you want to be first in values such as love, generosity or moral excellence. Jesus told James and John that his kingdom was not of this world. In his kingdom, he that is the greatest among them shall be the one who serves, and he that would be the chief would be the servant of all. What a deeply penetrating message that is to us! We are actually elevated through service. It would pay us all who are messengers of Jesus Christ and his followers to always keep this in remembrance. What drives the casino age message of the gospel is selfishness. It is a message that is completely and exclusively centered on pleasing the desires of the flesh. A message espousing the importance of obtaining material prosperity, places a premium on hoarding and covetousness. This is problematic because the first requirement of discipleship is self denial: "Then Jesus said to his disciples, If anyone would come after me, he must deny himself and take up his cross and follow me" (Matthew 16:23).

The Message of Christ is Characterized by Signs

One of the things that characterize this casino age message of prosperity is an emphasis on signs and miracles. Phrases like "Get your healing," "Get your financial breakthrough," and "Get ready for your harvest," are used to suggest that we can expect something from God if we just exercise the right kind of faith. Sow a seed, they say, and God will grant you a miracle. To accept this premise is to also suggest that God has to prove he is God and that he is less than God if he does not choose to grant a miracle. The important thing about the written word of God is that God in Christ no longer has to prove himself, for when he was here on earth, his miracle working signs and wonders served as the genuine proof of his authority as Christ.

The ministry of Jesus is filled with miracles and supernatural events. From the very beginning we find miracles in the ministry of Jesus - changing water to wine at a wedding at Cana of Galilee, feeding five thousand men beside the women and children and others. One day a woman who had an infirmity for twelve years fashioned in her mind that if she could just touch the hem of his garment, she could be made whole, and she was. In Matthew 4, Jesus healed every kind of disease and every kind of sickness among the people by some just touching the fringe of his cloak, and as many as touched it was being cured. Among the miracles were blindness, deafness, paralysis, fever, leprosy and others.

It cannot be questioned that there were many signs and miracles within the ministry of Jesus. It must be understood, however, that the miracles of Jesus were signs to authenticate that he was indeed the Messiah. None of the miracles of Jesus were primarily done for the purpose of relieving suffering though he had compassion and wanted to relieve suffering. The primary purpose of his miracles was to prove and reveal that He was the Messiah who was promised of God. The Apostle John records in Chapter 9, the miracle performed to one who was born blind. When the disciples saw him, they asked Jesus a question, *who did sin, this man or his parents that he was born blind?* Jesus said to them, *neither him nor his parents but that the works of God would be made manifest through him.* Jesus giving sight to this man at that point in history was to reveal to the disciples and others that he was indeed the Christ.

The New Testament was not yet written in the time of Jesus so to establish and corroborate the authenticity of Christ and the message of the kingdom, miracles were necessary. John, the Beloved Disciple, captures it well, "Jesus performed many other signs in the presence of his disciples, which are not recorded in this book. But these are written that you may believe that Jesus is the Messiah, the Son of God, and that by believing you may have life in his name" (John 20:30-31). The writer of Hebrews adds further insight on this matter in Chapter 2:3-4, "How shall we escape, if we neglect so great salvation; which at the first began to be spoken by the Lord, and was confirmed unto us by them that heard him; God also bearing them witness, both with signs and wonders, and with divers miracles, and gifts of the Holy Ghost, according to his own will?"

The Message of Christ is Characterized by Selflessness and Self Denial

The one thing that is unquestionably true about Jesus and his coming to earth is that it was a selfless act. The best depiction of this fact is recorded in Philippians 2:7 which says, "But made himself of no reputation, and took upon him the form of a servant, and was made in the likeness of men: And being found in fashion as a man, he humbled himself, and became obedient unto death, even the death of the cross". The Greek word that describes what Jesus did is *kenosis,* which means *emptied himself.* Indeed Jesus emptied himself of his divine nature, abandoned his sovereignty and left heaven and came to earth, voluntarily setting aside his God-like attributes. He set aside his omnipotence, omniscience and omnipresence. The old Baptist preacher would paint the picture this way: "He stepped out of eternity into time, boarded Mary's nine-month nature train, rode that train to a little place called Bethlehem, Judea, and there was born in the stable, wrapped in swaddling clothes and laid in a manger."

The Apostle John in John 1:14 says, "And the Word was made flesh, and dwelt among us, (and we beheld his glory, the glory as of the only begotten of the Father,) full of grace and truth." Our Lord gave it all up because he was willing to do the will of his Father, that is, to become the sacrificial lamb that humanity might have the opportunity to life everlasting. Beyond the aforementioned, his conduct within the frame of a human body is also revealing of his selflessness. He was able to resist the natural temptation of the flesh and yield to the will of his Father. We know he was tempted because the writer of Hebrews 4:15 says, "For we have not an high priest which cannot be touched with the feeling of our infirmities; but was in all points tempted like as we are, yet without sin."

We see his battle for victory over the flesh in the wilderness experience, which he had against the temptations of Satan. Essentially, he had to deny himself and embrace the cause of his Father. He denied the urges of hunger when

Satan said to him after he had fasted 40 days and nights "If you are the Son of God, command these stones to be made bread and he exclaimed, Man shall not live by bread alone but by every word that proceedeth out of the mouth of God" (Matthew 4:3-4). He resisted the urge of pride in refusing to test God as Satan took him to Jerusalem and sat him on the pinnacle of the temple, (the highest point) that overlooked the lowest valley, 700 feet from the ground and said to him, "if you are the Son of God, cast yourself down and you won't be hurt for the angels will bare you up that you would not touch the ground." Jesus' reply to Satan's contextual misapplication of the word was simply this, "thou shalt not tempt the Lord thy God." The third time he resists the temptation of fame and fortune as Satan took him to a high mountain and showed him all the kingdoms of the world and said, "All of this I will give you if you would just bow down and worship me." Jesus boldly proclaimed, "It is written, thou shalt worship God and him only shall thou serve." Self-denial was the key to his victory and is prevalent throughout the ministry of Jesus; he resisted the urge of those who followed him to make him king when his kingdom would not be of this world.

The Message of Christ is Characterized by Submission to the Father's Will

The two most significant acts of Christ's self denial can be seen during his last hours alive on this side of Calvary as he submitted to the **Will** of his father. The first obviously was when he went to the Garden of Gethsemane with his inner circle disciples asking them to watch as he went to pray. James Weldon Johnson pictures this moment by saying "The sweat was like drops of blood upon his brow" as he prayed, "Father, this bitter cup let it pass from me." Obviously, in his humanity, what he was about to go through as he saw it, was undesirable. The pain and the agony would be excruciating. Rather than resigning himself to his own **Will**, he said, "nevertheless not my will but your will be done." The second act of self-denial took place when he was arrested, tried before

Herod, Pilate, the Sanhedrin, then tied to a cross and demanded to go to Golgotha. There he was hung on that cross as he heard a dying thief and someone from among the unsympathetic crowd yell at him words that were reminiscent of Satan in the wilderness, "If you be the Son of God, get off this cross and save yourself." Had he chosen to come down, he would have been done with the agony and ascended back to glory, but he had emptied and denied himself because the will of the Father was paramount. Shouldn't our cause be the same, that is, to make the will of the Father the center of all we do in ministry? Like Christ, we must be emptied of self and deny urges of the flesh. Deliverance, breakthrough, health, wealth and prosperity, should not consume our mental faculties because in the final analysis these concerns are not to be ours anyway. "Be anxious for nothing. Our Father knows what we have need of even before we ask" (Matthew 5:32). If we embrace his will, he will surely provide for our needs.

The Message of Christ is Characterized by Stewardship

Contrary to what the purveyors of the prosperity doctrine may espouse, the Bible does not advocate "Name it and claim it" per se, but it does support the idea of being a good steward of material substance the Lord has blessed us with. Blessings referred to as a financial breakthrough, harvest or increase, does not result from an invocative incantation using false faith, but gifts given by God based purely on the basis of his grace. He is the giver and our responsibility is to be a good steward. Again Luke 6:38, a verse that is often used to promote seed sowing says, "Give, and it shall be given unto you; good measure, pressed down, and shaken together, and running over, shall men give into your bosom. For with the same measure that ye mete withal it shall be measured to you again." When you read the full context surrounding this verse, again, we can clearly see that what Jesus is really advocating is stewardship as opposed to seed sowing, depending on how the phrase seed sowing is used. Seed sowing used to imply an act of manipulating God and acting outside of his will, is faulty. However, having grown up on a farm, I understand the real principle of seed sowing. Seeds are sown but there is stewardship involved during this process.

The principle of stewardship is clearly shown in the parable of the good steward that Jesus gives in Matthew 25. A parable is a made up story to teach a heavenly kingdom principle. Jesus sets forth the principle in this parable that financial increase is due first of all to the goodness of God, and secondly, to a determined effort that we are willing to put forth. The parable speaks of a certain traveling man who summons all of his servants to him and gives them a certain amount of money, which in this case is called talents. To one he gives five, to the other two, and still another one. The traveling man, who represents the Lord, gives to these individual servants according to what he determined their ability to be.

These servants, metaphorically, are really representatives of the followers of the Lord, those who are a part of kingdom work. There are certain particulars within this parable that can be applied broadly in that they show us what God's expectation is relative to how we handle wealth that he has placed in our possession. The talents were given with the implicit understanding that they were to be used wisely and if one were to expect an increase, effort had to be made. Clearly, the traveling man here gives out of the abundance of his heart not because they deserved it necessarily, but because he was just good. He dispenses this money as he sees fit to do so. After all it is he who knows the servants better than anyone else. He knows how faithful they have been and how committed they have been in the past, or whether they have been careless with property that he had entrusted in their care before. Since these gifts were given out of the abundance of his heart, obviously, there should have been a degree of gratefulness on the part of the servants because they were given freely that which they did not have initially. How thankful ought we to be for all that God has blessed us with and what he has given us freely out of the plentitude of his heart.

The talents and how the traveling man chose to dispense them could have created a recipe for conflict. The one who was given five could have taken a high-minded attitude because he had more than the others, but that would have been the wrong attitude to have because the talents were given to him. It was unmerited favor. The master owed him nothing but entrusted him with his own wealth. The one who received the two talents could have taken the attitude of anger and resentment because he did not get as much as the one who received five. Again, that would not have been appropriate because he started with zero. Beyond these two, he who received the one talent could have just taken an apathetic view of life and said, "I don't care" or "anyway the wind blows is cool with me."

From all indications, that is exactly what he did. Later in the parable, Jesus tells us that the traveling man returned and called all of the servants to whom he had given gifts to account for the gift he had been given. Two had invested their money wisely and had gotten a good return on it. The one who was given five talents received five additional and the one who had two likewise received two additional talents. But on the other end of the spectrum, the servant who received one talent was angry and had no faith, initiative, or vision. He went and hid his talents in the earth in an effort to hold on to them for fear of losing what he had. The meaning of this parable is quite clear. We are only stewards of what the Lord places in our possession. He doesn't bless us with money or material for the purpose of hoarding or to satisfy our lustful appetites. This is not the type of behavior he rewards, but that which is exemplary of wisdom and diligence.

The message is completely opposite of what the doctrine of modern prosperity preaching advocates. In the early part of our discussion, I stated that one of the flaws of the Casino Age doctrine is that it undermines the work ethic while promoting the idea that one can just "Name it and Claim it," making demands of God that are not within **His Will** to do. It completely tosses away the mandate that God places on every able-bodied human to work to achieve success. A good work ethic is about behavior and being responsible. Responsibility, where the gifts of God are concerned, whether they are financial or spiritual, is extremely important. Bad behavior that is bred by laziness will result in an unproductive outcome. "The sluggard's craving will be the death of him, because his hands refuse to work" (Proverbs 21:25). We cannot "Name and Claim" our way out of what we have behaved our way into. God looks for a behavioral change as opposed to supplying us with everything we want regardless of whether we have the disciplinary wherewithal to handle what he gives us.

The Character of the Message of Christ

Points of Emphasis

- The Message of Christ is characterized by the ministry and life of Christ.

    - The ministry of Christ is a depiction by service and those who follow him must embrace the role of a servant. Mark 10:32-34

    - The ministry of Christ is supported by signs, but only to authenticate his divinity. John 20:30-31

    - The ministry of Christ is characterized by selflessness and self denial. Philippians 2:7

    - The ministry of Christ was defined by a submission to the Will of God. We who follow him must be willing to resist the will of the flesh and embrace the "His Will" believing that he will provide for our needs. Matthew 5:32

    - The ministry of Christ was characterized by his teachings on stewardship. It is behavior that is exemplary of responsibility and accountability that the Lord rewards. Matthew 25:14-30

Chapter VIII
Getting Back On Message

Returning to the Script

I thought that this would be an interesting title for this section as we journey toward the end of this book. "Flip the Script" is an urban colloquial expression that I sought to find the meaning of but found it rather difficult to do so. Since it is an urban expression, it dawned on me that the logical thing to do was to seek out an urban dictionary. I found that "Flip the Script" actually has several meanings. The term is used to suggest something that is unexpected or to deviate from the norm. Another definition describes the phrase as something commonly used in rap battles. It means to take what somebody said against you and use it against him or her.

Additionally, the definition suggests a matter of gaining control in a dialogue that is being dominated by another person so that you are now in charge. There were others that I found, but one that particularly meets our need for this discussion is the youthful definition, "to turn the tide, blaze a new trail, or otherwise go against a pre-established or preconceived idea, rule, norm, or expectancy." The operative word here is "script", which is used to form a larger word and that is "manuscript". Anyone who has done an extemporaneous speech, lecture, acted in any kind of play or presented a sermon that is not done from memory will be familiar with a manuscript. It is used to control the message that is being delivered, and when one veers from the manuscript or script, one is "off message." Essentially, what I have been making an effort to say in the previous chapters of this book is that messengers have gotten off script. Though I don't advocate flipping the script, we absolutely must return to the script.

Many who proclaim the gospel message of Jesus Christ have either purposely or accidentally strayed, and if the cause of Christ will be redeemed, it is necessary to remember that his cause cannot be separated from his message. His message is the only script that we are to concern ourselves with proclaiming. If it is not his message, it is the wrong script and promotes a perspective or philosophy of ministry that is not Christ centered. The Casino Age message is a different script that sweeps people up into a game of false promises and exploitations. How shall we return to a more sound and upright position with regard to what we advocate about how we are to view ministry? I have done my best to shed light on what I perceive to be the flawed doctrine of health, wealth and prosperity preaching which is based on self satisfaction, and slights experiences of hardship, troubles or trials as being a part of the Christian maturation process.

Is The Lord Enough?

In God's scheme of things, it has been his will from the very beginning to raise a people unto himself to carry his name throughout the earth. He began with Abraham to establish a relationship with him and ultimately from this patriarch raise up a nation that would make him the central focus. Why was this God's purpose? The Garden of Eden incident created what I like to call a "Divine Problem" that would ultimately be solved at Calvary. The sin in the garden by the first human beings God created, essentially divorced them from God, and consequentially, the entire human race. The holiness of God cannot tolerate the presence of sin, but the cross is the place where reconciliation is made.

When Jesus, hanging between the heavens and the earth, gave up the ghost, reconciliation was made for sinful mankind. The process toward that reconciliation however did not begin at the cross but in the Old Testament with Abraham, the Father of Faith. Abram, as he was originally named, was not seeking God but was called "to leave the land of his father and kindred and go to a land God would show him"—the "promised land" of Palestine. Without apprehension or question, Abram obeyed and went as God commanded. Through his obedience and faith in God, Abraham became the "father of the faithful." To him God made the promises of both the nation of Israel and the extending of eternal salvation to all nations of the world to come through Jesus Christ.

The Lord himself would be enough and provide for every need. This nation "the Children of Israel" that God raised up to himself through Abraham, were enslaved for more than 400 years in the land of Egypt under the hard taskmasters of Pharaoh. God sent the deliverer, Moses, and led them out the land with the use of his rod and miracles wrought by the Almighty. When they reached the Red Sea with Pharaoh's army closing in behind, they murmured at Moses in anger because they had no faith and that they would, at the sword of Pharaoh, perish. God showed his strong hand again by sending a blast from his nostrils while they slept at night and an east wind blew the waters asunder, and by day, they were able to all cross over on dry shod. All of the hosts of the Egyptian army were drowned. They then journeyed for three days to the wilderness of Shur where they found no water. "When they came to a place called Marah, where they could not drink the water there because they were bitter, they murmured again at Moses saying, 'What shall we drink?'" (Exodus 15:23-24) Moses cried to the Lord again and he was led to cut a branch from a tree and throw it into the water and the waters were made sweet.

God continued to show his strong hand of provision as they wandered in the wilderness for 40 years and wore clothes that never got old on their backs. When they wanted water, God brought water from a dry rock. When they wanted bread to eat, God rained down manna from heaven. Interestingly, when God gave them manna, he gave specific instructions that they were not to take any of the manna into their camps to save it or it would rot. When they got tired of the bread, God sent expensive quail into the camp. What God was teaching them through his provisions was that they should totally rely on him for their daily bread. All they needed was him, he was enough.

Earlier, I expounded on the compassionate heart of David toward Mephibosheth, the descendent of Saul. David is a prime example of one who knew that we were well off when God is the center of our affection. We know that David's sincere desire was to please the heart of God. Whenever he was confronted with his flaws or his frailty, he was always repentant and heavy hearted because he had failed God. Out of all of David's exploits and the things that we know about him written in scripture, the one thing that he is noted best for is the famous 23rd Psalm, "The Lord is my shepherd." It is perhaps the favorite of most people who are lovers of the word of God. I believe that David reflects back on the long journey of his life and recalls all of the ups, the downs, the valleys, the troubles, the trials and thinks about how God brought him through all of it.

The best metaphor David finds to express what he feels about God's provisional care is that of a shepherd. In the Psalms, he expresses that we should have a total reliance on the Lord and that the Lord should be central to our trust. David does not say that he relied on wealth and riches, though he was a wealthy man, of fame and status, though he was famous by virtue of being the King of Israel. He says "The Lord is my shepherd and I shall not want." I don't know what you gather from these words but this preacher hears David saying to us that we should not be consumed by our reliance on the substance of this world for fulfillment. To the contrary, we should be consumed by our love and dependence on the Lord, who is our shepherd, because in him we find everything we need.

It almost seems as though David is speaking to another sheep. Imagine if you will two sheep in separate but adjoining pastures. One sheep walks over to the fence and engages the other sheep in a conversation. He says to the other sheep, I have been watching you and I'm concerned because you look frail, anxious and down. I hear you at night walking around losing sleep as if you are distressed about what tomorrow will bring. While I don't want to get into your business, the sheep continues, I think that you have shepherd problems and I thought this would be a good opportunity to do some public relations work for my shepherd. While I don't know who your shepherd is, says the sheep, "the Lord is my shepherd and I shall not want." I shall not want for rest at night; I shall not want for food to eat; I shall not want for anything, because my shepherd takes care of me and he is the absolute center of my life. He leads me beside the quiet streams that relieve any stressful situation. Whatever I have lost as a result of the journey that we have been traveling together, he makes sure that it is restored. He guides and directs me for his name's sake because after all, it is about his name and reputation, not my own. I don't have to worry nor fear any evil thing that could befall me, because my shepherd is with me. What a beautiful picture David paints in Psalm 23 of a caring and loving God. When we make God enough, all of our needs will be met. He promised to meet all of our needs. Again, the thing that gives rise to the prosperity message is that people think the **Lord is not enough**. Many believe it suggests that one should seek to satisfy an insistent appetite for material things, but making materialism the central focus of one's affection consequently moves the Lord out. The truth is God has to be the center.

In the New Testament, God continues to meet the needs of his people through his son and our savior, Jesus Christ. Indeed Jesus is the central theme and all the miracles he performed were done for authenticating who he was and his relationship with God, the Father. His message to the masses was *Come unto me ye that labor and are heavy laden. I will give you rest* In other words, come, submit to me and your wellbeing becomes my responsibility. In John 14 he says, "I am the way, the truth and the life. No man comes to the Father but by me." In John 10 he says, "I am the door." In John 15 he says, "I am the true vine" and in John 10 again he says, "I am the good shepherd."

Again the troubling consequence of the health, wealth and prosperity doctrine or "Name It and Claim It," is that it essentially suggests that the major spiritual pursuit in our lives should be to possess material things as opposed to pursuing a relationship with Jesus Christ. It is his interests that should be primary as opposed to our own. Did not Jesus say himself,

"Seek ye first the kingdom of heaven and his righteousness and all these things shall be added unto thee." He also said, "One cannot serve two masters, either you will hate the one, and love the other or cleave to the one and despise the other. We cannot serve God and mammon."

One of the fastest growing fields in the country is that of counseling. Due to the frustration that exists within society today, college students are increasingly choosing counseling as a major. There seems to be as many Christians as there are non-Christians in need of counseling as a result of existing anxiety. Much of this frustration in the Christian world comes from a thwarted view of what the Christian life should be. Like Asaph in the 73rd Psalm, Christians are caught up with what they see in this physical world - the glamour, fame and fortune and consequently, develop a desire to be a part of it. Those who advocate a casino type message exploit that frustration by presenting Jesus as one who exists for the sole purpose of satisfying our appetite for materialism. The fact is that in this life there will be some occasional frustration. One having become a Christian does not exempt him from frustrating situations. The question is what will we do as a remedy? What we should not do is to yield ourselves to become exploited by those who are advocating false remedies for what troubles us. You will surely hear the words "If you want your healing, your deliverance, your breakthrough, a new car or even a house, just sow your seed and expect your increase."

The experience of Peter gives us a good picture of what we ought to do when we have lapses of frustration. The setting is along the Galilean Sea or otherwise known as Lake Gennesaret. Jesus is teaching a crowd of people, and it appears to be a rather large crowd. It seems that the people are so interested in the words of Jesus that they are pressing him out into the lake. Off at a distance, Peter, James and John, conspicuous in their absence from the crowd, were washing their nets. They were fishermen. The Bible does not give us a description of their demeanor, but in my mind's eye they are rather somber and don't appear to be happy. In fact, I would say they are frustrated. You see, they had been fishing all night and had not caught anything. When we focus back on Jesus and the crowd, we notice something quite interesting. Jesus uses Peter's boat as a kind of pulpit, and is shoved out into the water away from the people that he might have space to teach. Wow! Peter accedes to the Lord his boat. Well, perhaps the first thing we should do in the face of frustration is ***accommodate the Lord***. To accommodate him is really to make him the primary focus and the center of our activity. It is my experience that when we accommodate him, he will accommodate us.

As I just previously noted, in Matthew 6:33: "Seek ye first the kingdom of God, and his righteousness; and all these things shall be added unto you." Now, it is no small thing that Peter yields his boat to Jesus. Peter was a fisherman and his boat was his most important possession, yet he allowed Jesus the benefit of its use. Isn't that just the perfect metaphor for what the gospel message is all about? It is not about us but really about him. When Jesus finished his teaching of the crowd, he then focused his attention on Peter. Obviously, he was aware of their experience of not having caught any fish. He said to Peter in Luke 5:4, "Launch out into the deep and let your nets down for a catch."

The second thing we should do in dealing with our frustration is ***attend to the Lord's word***. Previously, I said that the health, wealth and prosperity message flourishes where there is a misapplication and misuse of scripture. Peter was told exactly what to do and he presented him with a decision either to obey or take another course. Thirdly, the challenge for Peter was to ***act on the Lord's word***. Acting on God's word actually activated his power. Peter said to the Lord, "We have toiled all night and have not caught anything, nevertheless at your word, we will launch out." This tells me that Peter had to fight in order to take this next step. He had to fight with the fact that he had been out all night and done all he could, yet was still unsuccessful. He had to fight with his own knowledge of how to fish. This was his occupation and his way of living, yet a man who is the son of a carpenter gives him instructions on how to fish. Peter humbly chose to put himself in the background and not allow his own intellectual pride, if you will, to take the center. He chose the words of Jesus and placed them as the foundation for his next steps forward.

If you have read the story, you know Peter launched out into the deep and the results were that he engulfed a multitude of fish. It was so miraculous that he had to call his other two partners, James and John, to bring their boats to help him because his net was inadequate. Scripture tells us that they not only filled Peter's boat, but James' and John's as well. What happened next is the most essential part of the story. After coming back to shore, Peter fell down at the feet of Jesus and acknowledges his divinity by calling him Lord. The response of Jesus really explains the purpose of the miracle. Jesus did not perform the miracle for the purpose of satisfying Peter's desire for fish but to meet a spiritual need in Peter and involve the three of them in the work of his ministry. He said in his response, "From now on you will fish for men as oppose to fishing for fish." Again the message of the gospel is not to raise the question of how much can we get from the Lord but to the contrary, how much are we willing to sacrifice for him and the cause of the kingdom.

The Truth About Trials
> "THEREFORE being justified by faith, we have peace with God through our Lord Jesus Christ: By whom also we have access by faith into this grace wherein we stand, and rejoice in hope of the glory of God. And not only so, but we glory in tribulations also: knowing that tribulation worketh patience; And patience, experience; and experience, hope: And hope maketh not ashamed; because the love of God is shed abroad in our hearts by the Holy Ghost which is given unto us. For when we were yet without strength, in due time Christ died for the ungodly" (Romans 5:1-6).

Haven't you heard people say things like, I'm really going through something right now or I'm having a lot of problems? After making such a statement they will ask the question, what's wrong with me? First, persons who make such statements and raise such questions have undoubtedly been fed faulty information. Sincere though they are, they are seriously in error in their understanding of the Christian's life relative to trouble and trials. They have obviously been taught that God is a kind of "I exist to make you feel good all the time kind of God." That's not so. Secondly, they may believe that the answer to prayer is always in the affirmative "yes." Thirdly, it may be that one's plight or predicament is always associated with something they have done wrong. That is not necessarily so. The Apostle Paul begins the chapter talking about the results of being justified by faith through Jesus Christ. He says that we have peace with God, access into his presence and we stand in his grace. What wonderful benefits we have in being justified by faith through Christ Jesus. But there are some less glamorous consequences that result from our being justified also. One of those consequences is that there will be certain trials.

    Trials are unavoidable if we are followers of Jesus Christ. Let us not lead anyone into thinking that if one lays down the ways of the world and embraces Jesus Christ, life from that point on is going to be with ease and everything positive, at least from their perspective. There will be some "necessary roughness" that we will have to endure in order to be a part of the Christian army. When we got saved, the Lord did not save us and take us to that wonderful city referred to in Revelation 21. That city where there is no more trouble, no more crying, no more dying and problems to deal with. He left us here on earth where evil people are and where we have to work by the sweat of our brows and where Satan runs free. The scripture says, "He goes to and fro seeking whom he may devour." Trials are not just inevitable but they also come in many forms. The saying is "If it is not one thing it's another and when it rains it pours." As soon as we get through dealing with one problem, another one comes. That's the way it is here. That's life and there is nothing we can do to change that. That's why we have to trust in God. The passage cited above reveals some profound truths about trials. Let's discuss them in the following sections.

Our Response to Trials

Paul says in Romans 5:3 "And not only so, but we glory in tribulations also: knowing that tribulation worketh patience." The apostle tells us to glory in our trials, which essentially means that we are to rejoice amid trials or tribulation. Rejoicing does not mean one has to jump up and down in jubilation and laugh hilariously because he is experiencing trials. Exhilaration in the midst of trials would not be sensible nor would it be an expression of what one really feels inside. No human being relishes trouble or embraces pain but they are usually things that we dread. Rejoicing necessarily means that one has an inner peace and satisfaction that though he is presently experiencing an undesirable situation, one knows that God ultimately is in charge. Since he is in charge, all will be well. Every Christian has the potential to rejoice through trials because all of us were given the peace of God when we met Jesus. In fact, Paul says in Romans 5:1 that we are justified by faith and because we are justified we have peace with God through Jesus Christ. This peace enables us at all times to know that our God is sufficiently able to handle whatever crisis we are confronted with. If I were in church, I would say, "An Amen goes right there!"

The Reason for Trials

The Apostle Paul gives us further insight into this matter of trials by telling us that they have their reasons for being prevalent in our lives. Indeed they have a purpose. "Trials worketh patience," Paul says. The word, patience, can best be described as endurance. Trials teach us how to endure because life is a series of crisis and challenges. Trials harden us up for those challenges so that we are able to go through them without breaking down or losing heart. I am an avid football fan and my favorite team is the Dallas Cowboys.

Every team in the National Football League loves to win and every team strives to ultimately play in that one final game of the season, which is the Super Bowl. If a team will be successful in gaining the victory, there is work that has to be put in during the week. They have to go through the rigors of training and I am sure it is not an easy process. They have to exercise and run plays so that when game time comes, they will be conditioned and able to execute that which they have practiced during the week. More often than not, the team that is in the best shape and works the hardest usually is victorious. So, through the rigors of trials, though they are sometimes uncomfortable, we learn patience that helps us persevere to victory.

     I have a saying, "God does not have any what-not children." A what-not is an unspecified object or article that is placed on a shelf solely for the purpose of being looked at. God did not create any of us for the purpose of just existing, but he intends for his children to be busy carrying out what his ordained purpose is for our lives. The trials of life in many instances help to shape us into what he intends for us to be. We see this in the life of Moses who was raised as an Egyptian but then was exiled for forty years and became a shepherd in the land of Jethro's Midian, leading sheep across the landscape and mountainside. It was there through the rigors of being a shepherd that God was training him to become the greatest leader in the history of the nation of Israel. Moses is just one example, but most of the patriarchs, prophets, men and women of God of the Old Testament endured trials of one kind or another to prepare them for the greater work of the Lord.

     Obviously in the New Testament, we would be hard pressed to find one major follower of Christ who did not endure trials because of their association with him. Trials not only produce the fruit of patience but patience yields experience. As a result of trails, one learns valuable knowledge about himself and what it takes to discipline one's self in the service of the Lord. Experience helps us to be a more authentic witness for the Lord. The saying is, "How do you know how I feel if you have not walked a mile in my shoes." It is quite easy for us to exclaim how strong we are in the Lord when things are going smoothly. It is another question all together, when we experience trials. In fact, have not we all been witness to others who were experiencing hardships or adversity and we gave them valuable advice about the goodness of God and how God will bring them through it? We even give scripture to support our advice. But then, we are confronted with similar circumstances, similar adversity, and the same advice we gave to a friend or associate who experienced hardship, we find difficult to embrace ourselves during trials.

Experience also helps us learn more about the character and nature of God. Most of us don't know the Lord quite as well as we feel we do. I would venture to say that Job's knowledge of God was far greater in the end, after having gone through his calamity than it was in the beginning. After experience has been manifested, hope is produced. Hope is not wishful thinking such as wishing I was rich, having the largest house or the nicest material things, but hope is confident expectation. It is a firm assurance regarding matters that may be unclear and even not known. It is what the righteous of the Lord holds on to and when one loses hope, he loses the meaning of life. The Apostle Paul says that the hope we have is based on the love that is shed abroad in our hearts through Jesus Christ and will not cause us to be disappointed. Our trust is in God for his protection, his provision and consequently, we need not be anxious or fret about anything. We will never be assured of being wealthy or ever be without some problems within our own bodies with regard to our health, but we can be assured that God will provide everything we need and that "all things work together for good to them that love God and who are the called according to his purpose" (Romans 8:28).

We remember Hannah of I Samuel Chapter One and Two, who had a husband, with another wife, Peninnah by name. Hannah was barren with no children but Peninnah had several. Peninnah often teased Hannah because Elkanah, the husband, favored Hannah. The Bible says, "The Lord had shut up her womb." Clearly, this was a sovereign act of God. This was not an act written by Satan, nor had Hannah done anything wrong to deserve her harsh treatment from the other woman. The Lord was using Hannah in a special way in his plan for his people Israel. One morning Hannah got up and went to church and poured out her heart before God in prayer as she said, "Lord, I want a man child." The priest thought she was drunk, but after praying she rose confidently with confirmation of an answered prayer. She went back home and in the fullness of time, Hannah had a baby boy and named him Samuel. She took him to the temple and gave him back to the Lord. Samuel became the first judge in the history of the nation Israel. I am sure you have known many Hannahs in one way or another. We have even been a Hannah at some point in our lives. God may have allowed "lack" in our lives to teach us how well he could provide, or momentary hardship as a means of taking us to a greater place of blessings. Through it all, we have learned to lean and depend on him.

Explaining Away Job

The most famous biblical story involving pain, suffering and evil is that of Job, the oldest book in the Bible. In it we see the providential hand of God working the events through and around Job's life. Many of those events caused Job a great deal of pain and suffering to which he raised the question to God, why? Those who advocate the health, wealth and prosperity gospel seek to explain away Job. Indeed they have a difficult time fitting him into the parenthesis of their teachings. Consequently, they blame Satan for all that goes on in the book of Job, and since it is Satan, they suggest what Job is experiencing cannot be, in their estimation, the will of God.

With my spiritual imagination, I can see Satan and all of his "imps" and "emissaries" sitting around in the first or the second heaven discussing the children of God and all the evil that they were considering bringing on various ones. One of them mentions the name Job, an interesting character who has great wealth, a great family and seemingly, great peace of mind. One may have said, "Let's give him trouble." Then another says, "It's impossible to do because we can't get to him." Perhaps Satan himself leaves that meeting and travels to the third Heaven, where he used to live. When he gets there he notices that God and his angels are in a meeting. When God sees him, God says, "From whence do you come?" Satan says "I have been traveling to and fro trying to find someone I can cause trouble." God says to him, "Have you thought about Job. He is righteous and there is nobody like him in the earth."

It is interesting that God brings up the name of Job to Satan and essentially offers him up for hardship and suffering. We should never believe that somehow things come upon us without the knowledge of the Almighty. Whatever adversity we will experience is allowed by God, because after all, he is sovereign and nothing sneaks by him. Satan responds to the Lord, "I have tried to get to Job but I'm having some difficulty because you have him fenced in and I can't quite reach him. If you would take down the fence and allow me at him, I will show you that he is not as faithful as you think he is. Indeed I will make him curse you to your face."

Satan, having gotten permission from God to test Job, commenced an assault on Job in a most severe way. He attacked him in the area of his ***possessions*** first. Job had 7,000 sheep, 3,000 camels, 500 yoke of oxen and 500 she-asses, and all were gone in a very short time. Imagine a Texas farmer today with thousands of heads of cattle having undergone a similar situation as Job. It would make the headlines of every newspaper, be the number one story on every evening news broadcast, and be a major story on the Internet around the world. Such calamity would be absolutely unheard of but that was just the tip of the iceberg for Job. Job possessed ten wonderful children that he prayed for constantly. From all indications, they were a close-knit family, and it seems to be that the siblings had continual communion together. They were eating at their brother's house and a horrific storm came and killed them all at once. Here is a man who has lost his livestock and now his children, yet he finds it within himself to worship God. In his own words, "The Lord giveth, the Lord taketh away. Blessed be the name of the Lord."

The one thing that we can always say about Satan is that he is persistent and never gives up. He was not able to make Job break under the pressure of losing all of his possessions so he inflicted him in the area of his *person* - his body. Emerods were protruding from his skin all over his body, from the crown of his head to the soles of his feet. Yet Job maintained his integrity and refused to bow to what Satan intended for his life. Finally, Satan assaulted him in the area of his ***personal relationships***. Job had a wife and three friends, Bildad, Zophar and Eliphaz. In times of trouble one expects that the person that one is married to would give support, but in Job's case, it was not to be. His wife, having to deal with a sick man that she had to take care of, and one with no longer the riches that he once possessed, gave in and suggested about and directly to Job that he would do the unthinkable, curse God and get it over with. Instead, Job responded with words that are among the most memorable in the book of Job, "You sound like a foolish woman." His friends abandoned him and accused him of secret sin and not having an effective prayer life or being the man that they thought he was. Despite all of these challenges, Job remained firm in his convictions. He questioned and even argued with God because he couldn't understand why he was experiencing what he was enduring, but he never gave up on God. Consequently, after having endured the test, God rewarded Job in the end with double what he had in the beginning.

The point that should be made here is that the health, wealth and prosperity doctrine seeks to explain away the struggles and challenges of Job by suggesting that it was conclusively the acts of Satan that were responsible. To explain it any other way would undermine the doctrine itself. Adversity, struggles, even suffering is never the will of God and does not fit into the framework of this doctrine. That is just not the case nor is it the true picture of what happened in the story of Job. Quite clearly, it all began with a sovereign

God who always reserves the right to himself to do as he wills. It is not really told in the book of Job why God chose to allow it, probably only Job knew. But isn't that the case with you or me who sometimes have to endure hardships? We don't always understand why at that moment but ultimately his will is revealed to us.

The Casino Age message presupposes a Christian's life to be one that is so narrow and simple as to only require satisfaction of the outer man, and that God does not have any requirements relative to the growth and development of the inner man. This faulty message suggests that all we need be concerned with is health, wealth and "naming it and claiming it," without pausing to consider that spiritual growth is the paramount thing with God. It suggests that it is God's pleasure to meet every desire of ours as if he is a vending machine waiting to be manipulated. There are times when we can neither name or claim when God purposes to do what he determines to be best. Adversity is often used by God to help mature us and develop our character and make us better witnesses for the kingdom.

There are times when God has divinely purposed that our plight and predicament are what is necessary for our own spiritual growth. Yes, his will may be that we are placed in a certain box at a certain period in time because it is best for us. What may this box consist of? It may, momentarily, consist of a person having to endure something that is most uncomfortable. It may be a job loss, losing a loved one, and yes, a health dilemma that he may ultimately get you through. Whatever the situation we are confronted with, God will inevitably work out for your good. There is a song that may be appropriate to recall here:

> "I don't know why I have to cry sometimes. I don't know why my poor heart bleeds sometimes but I know there's going to be a perfect day when troubles get out my way. I don't know why but I'll find out by and by. You know the Lord, he moves in mysterious ways. His wonders are to perform.

He plants his footsteps way out on the sea and rides on every storm. I don't know why God lets some things happen to me but I'll find out by and by."

The important thing that all of us should remember is that we belong to God. He is the creator and we are the creature, and whatever state we find ourselves in, we should seek to glorify him.

Jesus, Our Perfect Example

I rambled through my mind to determine how I would end this book and I thought I would do it by calling our attention to Jesus who is the head of the church, and the one in whom we are responsible to in this ministry. Every God-called preacher, pastor, minister or carrier of the word of God can think back to that time when you were called into the ministry of Christ. We were uncertain about a lot of things regarding the future, but there was one thing that we were certain of at that time, and that was we were called by the Lord to carry the gospel of Jesus Christ. After having submitted ourselves to much study and training, we ultimately came into the realization of the particular type of ministry that we would be involved in. Many of us have committed ourselves to our particular task. Indeed we consider ourselves on assignment for the Lord. When we consider our Savior, Jesus Christ, we understand clearly that he was also on assignment. Paul tells us in Philippians that we are to have the mind of Jesus Christ.

> "Let this mind be in you, which was also in Christ Jesus: Who, being in the form of God, thought it not robbery to be equal with God: But made himself of no reputation, and took upon him the form of a servant, and was made in the likeness of men: And being found in fashion as a man, he humbled himself, and became obedient unto death, even the death of the cross" (Philippians 2:5-8).

Yes, he was on an assignment to give his life as a ransom for humanity. If in ministry we ever get to the point where we lose our focus or somehow forget about what our fundamental task ought to be, we can always correct ourselves by looking at Christ and what he did when he was here. He is our perfect example. Jesus did not concern himself with his own interests. Indeed he left Heaven with all of its grandeur and glory to come to the mundane shores of planet earth, and it is evident by his own ministry that his concern was humanity and not himself.

> "And Jesus went about all the cities and villages, teaching in their synagogues, and preaching the gospel of the kingdom, and healing every sickness and every disease among the people. But when he saw the multitudes, he was moved with compassion on them, because they fainted, and were scattered abroad, as sheep having no shepherd. Then saith he unto his disciples, The harvest truly is plenteous, but the labourers are few; Pray ye therefore the Lord of the harvest, that he will send forth labourers into his harvest" (Matthew 9:35-38).

When it all boils down to it, isn't it really about the souls of men? Isn't it really about sharing the gospel of Jesus Christ to ensure that they will have eternal life? I believe that the most important word mentioned in the passage above is the word "compassion." If one does not have compassion, he will never be moved to embrace the cause of men. Compassion – that thing that refers to deep emotional feelings of one's bowels that plunges one into action. I challenge us to look beyond ourselves. Look at the field and you can see that men and women, boys and girls, are right for the harvest. "Pray to the Lord of the harvest, says Jesus that he might send forth labourers in the vineyard." My friends, we are those whom he has sent. The Lord has no hands but ours, no eyes but ours, and no legs or feet but ours. If we cannot look beyond ourselves, and if we are consumed with our own insatiable appetites to satisfy our fleshly desire for materialism and fame, the work of Christ will suffer. Perhaps the words of this old familiar hymn say it best:

> "How to reach the masses, men with every birth, for an answer, Jesus gave the key: And I, if I be lifted up from the earth, will draw all men unto me."
>
> "Oh, the world is hungry for the Living Bread, Lift the Savior up for them to see; Trust Him and do not doubt the words that He said, I'll draw all men unto me."
>
> "Don't exalt the preacher, don't exalt the pew, preach the gospel simple, full and free; Prove Him and you find that promise is true, I'll draw all men unto me."
>
> "Lift Him up; Lift Him up, Still He speaks from eternity: And I, if I be lifted up from the earth, Will draw all men unto me."

It's fitting and proper. After all, he is the Savior of the World. Amen.

Getting Back On Message
Points of Emphasis
- The central message of the Bible, Old and New Testament, is that God is in the center of his people and is enough to meet all their needs.

- The Health, Wealth and Prosperity message misrepresents the truth about trials.

- Trials are unavoidable for believers and work God's will by helping us mature and develop patience. Romans 8:53

- Adversity in our lives is sometimes permitted by God for his own sovereign purpose as in the life of Hannah and Job.

- The example of Christ gives us clear guidelines as to what our concern ought to be as his followers, that is the souls of humanity. Matthew 9:35-38

Endnotes

Alcorn, Randy *Eternal Perspectives Ministries, Prosperity Theology* (2010) http://www.epm.org/resources/2010/Mar/25/prosperity-theology-excerpt-if-god-good/

Associated Press *Missing Florida lottery winner killed* - US News "Abraham Shakespeare, Missing Lottery Winner "http://www.msnbc.msn.com/id/34735011/ns/us_news-crime_and_courts/ (Jan 6, 2010)

Billman, Jeffrey C. Viva Las Jesus Mega churches are all about entertainment *Orlando Weekly*. October 13 2005

Carson, Clayborne & Peter Holloran *A Knock at Midnight: Inspiration from the Great Sermons of Reverend Martin Luther King, Jr.* (Warner Books)

Caudill, Edward *Darwinism in the Press: The Evolution of an Idea.* (Lawrence Erlbaum Associates 1989). 98-99

Cooper, Helen *the Canterbury Tales* (Oxford University Press. New York. 1996), 96

Dobson, James C. Ph.D. *"Gambling's Dirty Little Secrets"* Focus on the Family (1999) Quotes of Mark Twain *The best throw of the dice is to throw them away* (May 16 2014) http://www.bedwardfamily.com/Commentary/Quotes_Twain.htm

"Flip the Script http://www.urbandictionary.com/define.php?term=Flip%20The%20 Script

Hall, Elvina M. *Jesus Paid It All* (The National Baptist Hymnal 1977) Sondra Ely Wheeler *Wealth as Peril and Obligation, the New Testament on Possessions* 1995 (WM B. Eerdmans Publishing Company)

Jasper, William F. *"Ponzi, Madoff and the Fed"*, The New American 25. (January 5, 2009) 44.

Johnson, James Weldon, *The book of American Negro poetry: Johnson,* 1871–1938 (New York: Harcourt, Brace and Company), 22.

Johnson, James Weldon, *The book of American Negro poetry: Johnson,* 1871–1938 (New York: Harcourt, Brace and Company), 22.

Jones, Charles Price *I Am Happy With Jesus Alone"* His Fullness Songs (National Publishing Board of The Church of Christ Holiness USA 1977)

Meekis, Laurie *How Casinos Lure in Gamblers and Try to Keep Them There 10 Casino Gambling Tricks* (May 19, 2008) http://www.associatedcontent.com/article/767243/how_casinos_lure_in_gamblers_and_try.html?cat=11

Mote, Edward *Jesus Paid It All* (The National Baptist Hymnal 1977)

Oatman, Johnson *Lift Him Up* (The New National Baptist Hymnal) 1977

On Media *"I Have Decided to Make Jesus..."* June 9, 2012 http://www.allgospellyrics.com/?sec=listing&lyricid=3 332

Ruben, Douglas H. *Handbook of Managed Care for Inpatient to Outpatient Treatment.* Eric Berne "The Games that People Play (Praeger Publishers 1993) 33.

Retrieved May 8, 2013 Merriam Webster Dictionary In Merriam-Webster.com. http://www.merriam-webster.com/dictionary

Shapiro, Lila "The Psychology of Lotteries: Feeling Poor Makes People Want to Play" *The Huffington Post* February 5 2011

Skousen, Mark "Is Greed Good?." Ideas on Liberty. May 2000 51

Use this convenient order form to order additional copies either of the author's books

Fallen In Love, Fallen Out of Like
RECAPTURING THE FEELINGS THAT GOT YOU MARRIED

Christ or the Casino
THE ERROR OF THE PROSPERITY GOSPEL MESSAGE

Please Print

Name
_____

Address
_____

City _____ State _____
Zip _____
Phone (   )

_____ Copies of book @ 0000 each $ _____
Postage & handling @ $0.00 per book $ _____ Total amount enclosed $ _____

A portion of the proceeds will go to Danny Hollins Ministries to help Urban Youth Program. To get your autographed copy, mail your check or money order payable to:
Danny Hollins Ministries 155 Fairfield Drive Jackson, Ms 39206
For more information contact
Danny Hollins,
601/259-7646

For the prosperity gospel, God could be seen as The Vending Machine God: put in faith and out pops blessings – money, homes, cars, beautiful spouses, clever kids, good neighbors, big churches, and plush vacations.
Scot McKnight

CHRIST OR THE CASINO
THE ERROR OF THE PROSPERITY GOSPEL MESSAGE

This book was inspired as a defense of the greatest message the world has ever known; that is, The Gospel Message of Jesus Christ. The Apostle Paul says, "For I am not ashamed of the gospel because it is the power of God that brings salvation to everyone that believes;". Implicit in this verse is that when we preach this gospel, we expect people to believe it. Therefore, it is gravely imperative that we, who are proclaimers of this sacred message, do so without troweling off into the use of some formula that advocates selfish gain or to satisfy covetous appetites. All too often today, our Savior is being presented as one who exists to sate all of our materialistic longings. Like casinos that lure thousands with the hope of hitting it big, gospel carriers are perpetuating an erroneous and one sided message of "Health Wealth and Prosperity" at the exclusion of one of service, sacrifice and stewardship.

Danny Ray Hollins PhD has pastored several churches since 1984, and is founding pastor of Grace Inspirations Church, Jackson, Mississippi. He earned his Doctorate in Urban Higher Education and Leadership, Studies toward MA Religion, MS in Counseling and BS in Education. His literary works include: *The Black Church and the Black Community, Fallen In Love Fallen out of Like, in addition to lectures Bridging the Gap Between the Church and the Community. Building Relationships with Faith Leaders: Answering the Call of Violence against Women, and The Leadership Skills of Jesus.*

www.ingramcontent.com/pod-product-compliance
Lightning Source LLC
Chambersburg PA
CBHW071126090426
42736CB00012B/2027